CHOICES

UPPER INTERMEDIATE WORKBOOK
with Audio CD

ROD FRICKER

WITH ONLINE SKILLS BY MICHAEL HARRIS

CONTENTS

TOPIC TALK – VOCABULARY

1 Match the descriptions (1-6) with the correct relationships (a-g). There is one extra relationship.

1 Peter is my mum's new husband.
  _g_

2 Leo is my mum's new husband's son from his first marriage.
  ____

3 Tom's got the same mother as me but a different father.
  ____

4 Simon is my mum's father's father.
  ____

5 Keith is my mum's cousin's son.
  ____

6 Ellen is my father's brother's daughter.
  ____

a My stepbrother.
b My second cousin.
c My aunt.
d My half-brother.
e My first cousin.
f My great-grandfather.
g My stepfather.

2 Complete the sentences with the correct words. You can see the first letter of each word.

1 My cousins and I always have a real l_augh___ together.

2 My sister and I always h_____ each other out when we've got problems.

3 I like Cath because we share the same interests and t_____.

4 My brother and his friends all have a similar s_____ of humour.

5 It's important for friends to have a lot in c_____ .

6 My best friend and I are very l_____ to each other.

7 My mum and I are very c_____ .

8 My mum and dad t_____ each other completely.

9 My friend and his sister g_____ on brilliantly together.

10 Andy and I spend a lot of time together because we like each other's c_____ .

3 Choose the correct word.

CLASS 9C
Relationships survey
❤❤❤❤❤❤❤❤❤❤❤❤❤❤❤❤❤❤❤❤❤❤❤

Please answer the questions and give the survey to Melanie or Kim.

How often do you and your boyfriend/girlfriend:

1 _go_/stay/meet out together?
  About twice a week.

2 go/meet/look up and chat?
  Every day at school.

3 text together/yourselves/each other?
  All the time.

4 talk on/to/with the phone?
  Every day.

5 use a social network like Facebook to keep/meet/talk in touch?
  Every day.

Thank you!

4 Complete the text with the words below. There are four extra words.

~~big~~ close do few fond get girlfriend going keep lots met same similar together

I've got a ¹ _big__ family with ² _____ of cousins, uncles and aunts. I ³ _____ on especially well with my cousin, Richard. He lives near me and we ⁴ _____ lots of things together.
My ⁵ _____ is called Lucy. We ⁶ _____ when we were in Year 6 at school but we started ⁷ _____ out together when we were in Year 9. We get on well ⁸ _____ because we have a ⁹ _____ sense of humour but we don't have many things in common really. We are ¹⁰ _____ of each other. Are we in love? Maybe!

Reading

1 Read the text quickly and decide what it is about.

A Mobile phones should not be allowed in the school canteen.

B People who want to speak face to face should have separate tables to sit on in the school canteen.

C Loud ring tones make it difficult to communicate face to face in the school canteen.

An idea for the school canteen

Do you eat dinner at school? I do and so do many of my friends but there never seems to be anyone I can talk to. Everyone is using their mobile phone. The problem is so bad that last week I sat for thirty minutes with three of my best friends and I didn't say more than a few words to any of them. Every time I started a conversation, someone's phone would ring or a text would arrive. I was so annoyed. No one even apologised to me or switched their phone off. The conversation with me just stopped while they concentrated on the small piece of plastic held in their hands. It's strange because, when I'm not with them, they are always phoning or texting me. When we're together, though, they're always trying to get in touch with someone else. Perhaps the person they are with when they are busy phoning me! It was such a miserable half-hour that I nearly went to sit on a different table. I thought I could phone them and have a chat! Instead, I decided to write this article for the school newsletter.

I know there are a few other people who think like me and I believe it's up to us, the students, to do something about the problem. We don't need the teachers to do anything - it is our responsibility. That's why I propose setting up a 'no-phone' area of the canteen. We could then sit in that area and know that the other people would pay attention to us when we spoke to them. It would be a great place to meet new people and get to know them. I think we should start by making half the room a no-phone area. We could then see how popular each area is and make them larger or smaller if necessary.

I want to make it clear that I'm not against mobile phones or the noise they make. I love noise. My ring tones are all loud rock songs and, when I'm on my own, I get very excited when I hear the sound of my phone ringing. At home, in my free time, I often send texts or call my friends. When I'm at school, though, I don't need a phone because I'm with my friends. They are the people I want to communicate with and I can do that face to face.

If you agree, please email no_phonearea@yorkschool.co.uk

Thanks!

Stella Morgan Class 10C

2 Read the text again. Are the statements (1–8) true (T) or false (F)?

The writer believes that:

1 people should talk together more at lunchtime. _T_
2 her friends were rude to her when their phones rang. ___
3 her friends don't contact her enough when she's not with them. ___
4 some other students agree with her opinions. ___
5 the teachers should do something about the problem. ___
6 the non-phone users will need more room than the phone users. ___
7 loud ring tones are annoying. ___
8 mobile phones are great when you are alone. ___

Word Builder Multi-part verbs (1)

3 Replace the underlined words with a multi-part verb below.

get in the way of   get in touch with   it's up to us
pay attention to   put in place   take into account

1 Listen carefully to what he is saying about the dangers of mobile phone use.
   Pay attention to what he is saying about the dangers of mobile phone use.
2 No one is going to help us. We have to help ourselves.
   No one is going to help us. _____ to help ourselves.
3 How can I contact Maria?
   How can I _____ Maria?
4 The EU has set up new laws to reduce the cost of using mobile phones abroad.
   The EU has _____ new laws to reduce the cost of using mobile phones abroad.
5 Don't just think of yourself. You have to remember other people's feelings, too.
   Don't just think of yourself. You have to _____ _____ other people's feelings _____ , too.
6 Does your mobile phone use disturb your normal, everyday relationships?
   Does your mobile phone use _____ your normal, everyday relationships?

Sentence Builder Result linkers

4 Choose the correct word.

1 I was (so)/such tired that I fell asleep in front of the computer.
2 The train was so/such crowded that I had to stand for the whole journey.
3 I've got so/such a lot of work to do that I don't think I'll have time to go.
4 Silent carriages are so/such a good idea that I can't believe no one thought of them before.
5 I was so/such angry that I decided to tell the mobile phone user to switch off his phone.
6 Mobile phones are so/such an easy way to keep in touch that there's no reason to lose contact with anyone.

5 Complete the second sentence so that it has the same meaning as the first.

1 The jacket was so expensive that I decided not to buy it.
   It was _such an expensive jacket that I decided not to buy it._
2 We had such a long conversation that I forgot to get off the train.
   Our conversation was _____ _____
3 This is such a complicated phone that I don't really know how to use it.
   This phone is _____ _____
4 The children were so quiet that I forgot that they were there.
   They were such _____ _____
5 It was such a loud concert that we couldn't hear each other speak.
   The concert was _____ _____
6 The woman on the train was so annoying that everyone else moved away from her.
   There was such _____ _____

GRAMMAR
Present and past tenses

Complete Exercises A–B before you start this lesson.

A Complete the sentences with the verbs in the tenses shown.

Present Simple

1 How often ___*does your mother talk*___ (your mother / talk) on the phone?

Present Continuous

2 What _____ (you / do) at the moment?

Present Perfect

3 You _____ (text) your boyfriend three times already today.

Past Simple

4 We _____ (go) shopping and _____ (buy) some T-shirts.

Past Continuous

5 I _____ (laugh) at a joke my friend told me when our teacher came into the room.

Present Perfect Continuous

6 They _____ (go out) for three months now.

Past Perfect

7 Until last week, I _____ (never / use) Skype.

B Complete the sentences with the correct form of the verbs in brackets.

Present simple and present continuous

1 A: Why ___*are you walking*___ (you / walk) to school today?

2 B: My dad usually _____ (take) me but he had to leave early this morning.

Present perfect and past simple

3 A: _____ (you / ever / be) on a date?

4 B: Yes, I _____ (go) out with Sarah last Friday.

Past simple and past perfect

5 A: Why _____ (you / not / come) to the cinema with us last weekend?

6 B: Because I _____ (already / see) that film.

Present perfect and present perfect continuous

7 A: You _____ (talk) on the phone all afternoon. How many friends have you got?

8 B: I _____ (only / talk) to three people but they're all very talkative.

Past simple and past continuous

9 A: Who _____ (you / wait) for when I _____ (see) you?

10 B: I (wait) _____ for Tom.

1 * Choose the correct verb form.

1 Elaine *never uses*/*is never using* Skype.

2 Who *do you go*/*are you going* out with at the moment?

3 *I've had*/*I'm having* a good idea. Do you want to hear it?

4 I *don't like*/*am not liking* speaking in public.

5 Emily *has never had*/*never has* a smart phone.

6 Sorry I'm late. I hope you *aren't waiting*/*haven't been waiting* long.

7 *I've lost*/*I've been losing* contact with all my friends from primary school.

8 I *think*/*I'm thinking* of deleting my Facebook account.

9 Steve *is*/*has been* a member of the school orchestra since January.

2 * Complete the sentences and questions with the words below.

~~did~~   did (x 2)   didn't   had (x 2)   said
was   wasn't   were   weren't

1 When _____*did*_____ you two first meet?

2 When it was time to pay for my meal, I realised that I _____ left my money at home.

3 Who _____ you waiting for when I saw you last night?

4 Why _____ you and Lisa split up last Saturday?

5 Why are you angry? We _____ doing anything wrong.

6 How many girls _____ your brother been out with before he met Charlene?

7 Why couldn't you get into the disco on Saturday?

I _____ wearing my old jeans and there's a 'no jeans' rule there.

8 I think there's something wrong with my computer. It _____ working properly last night.

9 What _____ you say to Rebecca when you first went over to talk to her?

I _____ 'Hi, nice T-shirt.'

10 I _____ know what to wear on my date so I asked on Facebook and got 103 suggestions.

3 ** Choose the correct answers.

1 When my mum and dad got married, they _c_ each other for three years.
  a have known
  b knew
  c had known

2 My cousin ___ a great website of chat-up lines.
  a finds
  b has found
  c has been finding

3 What time ___ home last night?
  a did you get
  b had you got
  c have you got

4 My brother ___ girls at all.
  a hasn't understood
  b doesn't understand
  c isn't understanding

5 ___ Jackie still ___ out with Mick?
  a Is / going
  b Has / gone
  c Does / go

6 When Susie phoned to say she couldn't go out, ___ two tickets for the cinema.
  a I'd already bought
  b I've already bought
  c I've already been buying

7 My friend ___ knowing all the latest gossip about people in our class.
  a is loving
  b has loved
  c loves

8 ___ for that boy to ask me for a dance for twenty minutes. If he doesn't ask soon, I'll go and ask him!
  a I waited
  b I'm waiting
  c I've been waiting

4 *** Complete the dialogue with the correct form of the verbs in brackets.

Matt: What's wrong?

Ben: I ¹_'ve had_ (have) an argument with Kate. I was late for our date yesterday. By the time I arrived at the cinema, she ²_____ (already leave).

Matt: Why were you late?

Ben: There ³_____ (be) a problem with my bus.

Matt: Why ⁴_____ (you not phone) her?

Ben: I ⁵_____ (not have) my phone with me. I ⁶_____ (sit) on the bus when it broke down and, when I ⁷_____ (look) in my pocket, it wasn't there.

Matt: So, ⁸_____ (you talk) to Kate today?

Ben: No. I ⁹_____ (try) to phone her all day. She always ¹⁰_____ (take) her phone to school. I'll try again.

Matt: There's no point. She ¹¹_____ (play) basketball at the moment.

Ben: Oh, no! I (promised) to go and watch her. Quick. Where ¹²_____ (they play)?

Grammar Alive Sharing personal information

5 *** Make questions and answers from the cues.

1 A: you work / at the moment?
  Are you working at the moment?
  B: ✓ / at a pizza restaurant
  Yes, I am. I'm working at a pizza restaurant.

2 A: How long / work there?
  _____
  B: work there / three months
  _____

3 A: you like it?
  _____
  B: ✓ / not have to / work too hard
  _____

4 A: What time / you start work?
  _____
  B: / at 10 a.m. but I / not finish until 8 p.m.
  _____

5 A: How / find out / about the job?
  _____
  B: My friend / tell me about it. He / work / there last year
  _____

6 A: you save / a lot of money since / start / working there?
  _____
  B: ✗ / but I / spend / a lot!
  _____

Oral Skills

Listening

1 〔1.2〕 **Listen to a talk about young people staying at home for longer. Match the numbers (1-4) with the facts (a-e). One number matches two facts.**

1 25 _d_
2 10 ____
3 2 ____
4 5 ____

a the percentage of men aged over thirty still living with their parents

b the number of years' wages the average house costs today

c the average age difference between men and women when they get married

d the percentage of men aged between 20-29 still living with their parents

e the percentage of women aged over thirty still living with their parents

2 〔1.2〕 **Listen again and choose the correct answer.**

1 In the past, the British tended to leave home ___ _a_
  a at an earlier age than most Europeans.
  b at the same age as other Europeans.
  c at a later age than most Europeans.

2 The proportion of women in their twenties still living with their parents is about _____
  a half the proportion of men.
  b double the proportion of men.
  c the same as the proportion of men.

3 It is less common nowadays for young people to _____
  a share accommodation with friends.
  b move in with a partner.
  c live alone.

4 Twenty years ago, house prices cost about _____
  a five times less than today.
  b three times more than today.
  c three times more than a person earned in a year.

5 It is difficult for young people to find _____
  a part-time work.
  b well-paid work.
  c temporary work.

6 Students are now more likely to _____
  a ask their parents for money.
  b study close to home.
  c be forced to give up their studies and return home.

Speaking

1 **Look at the presentation about going to university in different countries. Put the paragraphs (A-D) in the correct order.**

A ___
So, to <u>conclude</u>, there are more young people going to university each year. However, with costs rising, this [i] _trend_ may not continue into the future. So, that's [ii] _____ . Has anyone got any questions?

B ___
However, despite the high cost of education, there are more students at university than at any time in the past. One reason for this is that more and more jobs require university degrees nowadays. Also, wages for unskilled work have <u>gone down</u> while salaries for managers and professionals have <u>risen</u>.

C _1_
[iii] _____ this [iv] _____ , we're going to look at the number of people going to university in different countries. In some countries like Finland, the proportion is now over 80% whereas in the UK, the <u>numbers</u> are lower. <u>But</u> this is also a big increase over the last fifteen years.

D ___
Another [v] _____ to <u>discuss</u> is the cost of studying in different countries. In Scandinavia, university education is free. In England, the cost of studying <u>has gone up</u> from nothing in 1997 to a maximum of £9000 a year in 2012.

2 **Match the words and phrases (1-6) with the underlined words in the presentation that they could replace.**

1 comment on ___ _discuss_
2 increased _____
3 figures _____
4 summarise _____
5 decreased _____
6 However, _____

3 〔1.3〕 **Complete the presentation with one word below in each gap (i-v). Then listen to check your answers.**

it   talk   ~~trend~~   area   in

LESSON 4

GRAMMAR
Quantity

1 * Choose the correct word.

1 *No/None* of my friends uses Skype.

2 I get *several/a lot* emails every day.

3 Hardly *none/any* of these texts are important.

4 Invite Emily and Janice to your party. They *all/both* invited you.

5 Paul can pass his exams with very *little/few* effort. It's not fair.

6 Hurry up. We haven't got *many/much* time left.

7 *Most/Any* of my classmates have got Facebook accounts.

8 Don't help the boys with their homework. There are fifteen of them in the class and *none/neither* of them helped you.

2 * Complete the sentences with *few, fewer, little* or *less.*

1 I get *fewer* emails than texts.

2 There were _____ people at the party than I expected.

3 I can't buy a ticket for the concert as I only have a _____ money left.

4 My brother has very _____ good ideas.

5 You should spend _____ time playing games and more time reading.

6 You should eat more vegetables and _____ chips.

7 _____ of us understood the question.

8 My sisters spend _____ money on petrol now that they have bought new bikes.

3 ** Complete the text with one word in each gap.

Feeling better!

I often worried about not being allowed to go out very often. I thought [1]a*ll* my friends were enjoying themselves while I was stuck at home. Then, when I asked them, I found out that [2]m_____ of them were just like me, Two boys said they went out every night but I found out later that [3]b_____ of them were lying and [4]n_____ of them go out at all – not even at the weekend!

[5]H_____ a_____ of my friends go out between Sunday and Thursday. A [6]f_____ do but they have to be home before nine o'clock. [7]N_____ of my friends can stay out after ten o'clock during the week even if they want to go to a concert or a film.

At the weekend, things are more relaxed for [8]m_____ of us. We have more freedom on Fridays and Saturdays and [9]s_____ of us can even stay out until midnight. [10]N_____ parents allow their children to stay out all night, though, except when they are staying at a friend's house and the friend's parents are there to look after them.

Now I don't mind being at home because I know that I'm not missing any great parties.

Posted 25 minutes ago

4 *** Rewrite the sentences using the words in brackets.

1 The majority of people I know listen to MP3 players on their way to school.
(most) *Most people I know listen to MP3 players on their way to school.*

2 I've got hardly any work to do.
(much) _____

3 No teachers at our school let their students leave early.
(none) _____

4 I haven't got many Facebook friends at all.
(hardly) _____

5 A number of people I know are bored with Facebook.
(several) _____

6 I've got two brothers. They are very lazy.
(both) _____

7 I've got two phones. They don't work.
(neither) _____

Writing Workshop 1

1 Read the email quickly and match the people (1-5) with the information (a-e).

1 Ed _e_
2 Mark ___
3 Emma ___
4 Amy ___
5 Neil ___

a was Ed's girlfriend.
b might be Ed's new girlfriend.
c is in a band.
d lent someone a CD.
e lost a mobile phone.

From: Ed
To: Mark

Hi Mark,

Thanks for the email. Glad to hear your band is doing well. Let me know when you organise a concert and I'll definitely come and see you play. I need something to cheer me up. This has been a BAD week!

¹As you k_now_____ , I started going out with Emma last month. Unfortunately, we split up on Saturday. ²To be h_____ , I wasn't that upset because we didn't have a lot in common. ³In f_____ , there's another girl in my class called Amy who I really like and who I think likes me ☺.

⁴A_____ , the worst thing happened on Wednesday – I lost my new, expensive mobile phone!! My parents were very upset, ⁵e_____ when I told them that I had left it on the grass at school. No one handed it in so my parents rang the phone company and cancelled my account. So now I've got no phone. Well, ⁶a_____ , I have got one – a really old one from my dad that weighs a ton and doesn't even have any games on it ☹.

So, that's my week so far. They say that trouble comes in threes so I'm waiting for one more disaster to happen!

Write soon
Ed

Oh, ⁷b_____ the w_____ , I forgot to tell you. Neil asked me to say hello and he wants to know when you're going to give him his CD back.

---

2 Complete the email with one word in each gap.

3 Complete the ideas for Mark's reply to Ed with your own ideas.

Ed's love life
1 To be honest _____
_____

2 In fact _____
_____

Neil's CD
3 To tell the truth _____
_____

The band
4 It was really annoying, especially _____
_____

Other news
5 Oh, by the way _____
_____

4 Write an email from Mark to Ed. Use your ideas from Exercise 3 and the phrases from Exercise 2. Remember to include an introduction and a conclusion in your email.

- Respond to Ed's problems.
- Give a message to Neil about the CD.
- Tell Ed the latest news about the band.
- Invite Ed to a concert, film or party.

From: Mark
To: Ed

Hi Ed,
Thanks for the email.

Check Your Progress 1

1 Relationships **Match the beginnings (1-5) with the correct endings (a-e).**

1 We have a lot ___
2 My parents always tell us we should put ___
3 We are in ___
4 We've got a similar sense ___
5 It's important to be loyal ___

a love.
b to each other.
c in common.
d family first.
e of humour.

/5

2 Multi-part verbs (1) **Choose the correct words.**

1 You should take *into/on/for* account other people's feelings, too.
2 Pay attention *for/with/to* what your girlfriend tells you she likes and doesn't like.
3 The government is putting *on/in/at* place a new law to stop illegal downloading.
4 It is *up to/into/onto* all of us to make this world a better place.
5 Your relationship with Martin is getting *on/out of/in* the way of your friendship with me.

/5

3 Result linkers (1) **Make sentences from the cues using** *so ... that* **or** *such ... that.*

1 Gary / hard-working / always comes top in class tests

_____

2 I got / bad report / my parents stopped me from using my computer during the week

_____

3 Mike / good friend / tell him all my problems

_____

4 Jackie / popular / she gets invited to parties every week

_____

/4

4 Present tenses **Complete the sentences with the correct form of the verbs in brackets.**

1 I've lost my phone. _____ (you / see) it anywhere?
2 Why _____ (your brother / wear) those trousers? Is he going to a fancy dress party this evening?
3 David and Alison _____ (decide) to stop seeing each other.
4 My eyes hurt. I _____ (play) online games all day.
5 How long _____ (this film / last)?

/5

5 Past tenses **Complete the text with the correct form of the verbs below.**

be   see (x 2)   take   talk

I ¹_____ Rachel to the cinema last Saturday. By the time she arrived, I ²_____ there for about an hour. When she arrived, I ³_____ to my friend Jim on the phone. I suddenly ⁴_____ her standing there so I quickly switched the phone off. The film was OK. I ⁵_____ it before but I knew that Rachel wanted to see it.

/5

6 Quantity **Complete the sentences with the words below. There are three extra words.**

any   both   few   less   little   neither   none   lots   several

1 _____ of my parents like my music – they say it's just a noise.
2 You'll need _____ of money for the holiday so start saving now.
3 _____ of the people I phoned answered. Where were they all?
4 Hardly _____ of my Facebook friends every contact me.
5 My phone was expensive but it was _____ expensive than my brother's.
6 Very _____ adults really understand text speak.

/6

TOTAL SCORE   /30

Module Diary

1 Look at the objectives on page 5 in the Students' Book. Choose three and evaluate your learning.

1 Now I can _____
   well / quite well / with problems.
2 Now I can _____
   well / quite well / with problems.
3 Now I can _____
   well / quite well / with problems.

2 Look at your results. What language areas in this module do you need to study more?

Sound Choice 1

❶ **1.5** Grammar - contractions **Listen to the sentences and write the number of words you hear. Contractions are two words.**

1 _eight_	**3** ____	**5** ____	**7** ____
2 ____	**4** ____	**6** ____	**8** ____

❷ **1.6** Consonants - consonant clusters **Listen and complete the consonant cluster in each word.**

Beginning of the word	Middle of the word	End of the word
1 s _c h_ oolmates	**5** step _ _ other	**9** intere _ _ s
2 S _ ype	**6** frie _ d _ _ ip	**10** resear _ _
3 _ rend	**7** u _ _ l e	**11** te _ _ s
4 s _ orty	**8** at _ _ etic	**12** confli _ _ s

❸ **1.7** Vowels - long and short vowel sounds **Listen and tick (✓) the words you hear.**

1 bit	✓	beat	☐	**6** ant	☐	aunt	☐
2 look	☐	Luke	☐	**7** debt	☐	dirt	☐
3 am	☐	arm	☐	**8** pot	☐	port	☐
4 cot	☐	caught	☐	**9** sit	☐	seat	☐
5 bed	☐	bird	☐	**10** pull	☐	pool	☐

❹ **1.8** Spelling - double consonants **Listen to the words and write the letters which are doubled. Sometimes, more than one letter is doubled.**

1 _m_	**3** ____	**5** ____	**7** ____
2 ____	**4** ____	**6** ____	**8** ____

❺ **1.9** Spelling - double and single consonants **Listen and write the words in British English (BrE) and American English (AmE).**

BrE	AmE
1 _travelled_	_traveled_
2 _____	_____
3 _____	_____
4 _____	_____
5 _____	_____

❻ **1.10** Expressions - describing figures and trends **Listen to the sentences and repeat the underlined phrases.**

1 In this talk, we're going to look at education.

2 That figure is up by 50 percent since last year.

3 Another area to comment on is exam results.

4 The proportion of students getting an A grade has gone up to 33 percent.

5 The percentage of students going to university went up from 22 percent to 35 percent between 1995 and 2010.

6 The number of students leaving school at 16 has gone down, too.

7 Only one in nine students leaves school with no qualifications at all.

8 So, to summarise, grades are getting better and more students are going on to further education.

❼ **1.11** Difficult words - stress in compound words **Listen to the words and underline the stressed syllables.**

1 teammate

2 good-looking

3 social network

4 stepmother

5 well-known

6 single parents

7 hard-working

8 grandparents

TOPIC TALK – VOCABULARY

1 Complete the sentences (1-8). Then write the words in the puzzle.

We are campaigning for:

1 better ___healthcare___ - more doctors, better hospitals and free medicine.
2 better _____ - free universities, smaller class sizes and more.
3 _____ of speech.
4 _____ - no more war!
5 more spending on the _____ - special lifts, nurses to visit people in their homes
6 better _____ transport - cheap buses and trains.
7 human _____ .
8 care for the _____ - no more pollution, more recycling, clean energy.

¹h	e	a	l	t	h	c	a	r	e
		²				a			
³						m			
					⁴p				
		⁵			a				
	⁶				i				
			⁷		g				
⁸					n				

2 Look at the campaigns below. Rewrite the endings (1-8) with one word in each gap.

We are campaigning against:

1 children being poor. c_hild_ p_overty_
2 being nasty to animals. c_____ to animals
3 the raising of the Earth's temperature.
   g_____ w_____
4 people having nowhere to live. h_____
5 dirty air and water. p_____
6 reducing the amount of money spent on important services. s_____ c_____
7 treating people of different colour or nationality differently. r_____
8 officials accepting money or presents from people in return for making decisions which help those people.
   c_____

3 Match the verbs (1-6) with the correct words (a-f).

What did you do to try to change the world?
1 I attended _d_   a in fundraising activities.
2 I donated ___   b on demonstrations.
3 I went ___   c as a volunteer.
4 I signed ___   d meetings.
5 I took part ___   e petitions.
6 I worked ___   f money.

4 Complete the dialogue with the words below. There are four extra words.

~~against~~ agree approve as belong do in issues join NGO on protest support

Craig: We're going on a march tomorrow. We're campaigning ¹ _against_ street crime.

Wendy: Why? I ² _____ campaigns when the government does something wrong but I don't really ³ _____ of marching for no reason.

Craig: But there is a reason. We can show the government that we want them to do more to protect us.

Wendy: I think other ⁴ _____ are more important like spending cuts. And we should really ⁵ _____ more about poverty, then there would be less crime.

Craig: I agree, but the government is cutting spending on the police, too. What else can we do?

Wendy: You could join an ⁶ _____ . I ⁷ _____ to the Global Call to Action Against Poverty. It's a huge organisation. I've also worked ⁸ _____ a volunteer giving food to the homeless in my town. I've never been ⁹ _____ a demonstration but I try to do what I can.

Craig: Wow. I didn't realise. Let's go for a cola and you can tell me more about this organisation.

Wendy: Good idea. We can have a pizza if you want, too.

GRAMMAR
Talking about the past and Past Perfect Continuous

REMEMBER

Complete Exercises A–B before you start this lesson.

A Make questions and answers from the cues using the Present Perfect or the Present Perfect Continuous.

1 A: What / you / do all morning?
What have you been doing all morning?

2 B: I / read.
_____

Our teacher told us to read *Jane Eyre*.

3 A: How much / you read?
_____

4 B: I / read / 38 pages.
_____

5 A: you / play on your computer?
_____

6 B: No. I / write / emails.
_____

7 A: How many / send?
_____

8 B: I / not send / any. I / not finish / any of them.
_____

B Match the beginnings (1–5) with the correct endings (a–e) and put the verbs into the Past Perfect.

1 Our teacher was angry because we
hadn't done (not do) _b_

2 They were made homeless because they
_____ (lose) ___

3 There were no more whales left because people _____ (kill) ___

4 I went on a protest because the government _____ (cut) ___

5 Tom was very nervous because he
_____ (never be) ___

a them all.
b our homework.
c on a plane before.
d their jobs and didn't have any money.
e spending on the environment.

1 * Complete the sentences with the verbs below.

hadn't answered   hadn't done   ~~had been running~~
had arrived   hadn't eaten   hadn't phoned
had been thinking   had run   had started (x 2)
had been waiting

1 When I saw James, he was really tired. He
had been running . He _____
at 8 o'clock and, when I saw him, he
_____ 12 km.

2 When I saw Jane, she was really hungry. She
_____ anything for breakfast.
She _____ well in her English test
because she _____ about food the whole time.

3 When I saw Henry, he was really angry. He
_____ at the theatre early and he
_____ for Emily for an hour. The
play _____ but she still wasn't
there. She _____ him and she
_____ his phone calls to her.

2 * Complete the text with the verbs in brackets in the Past Perfect or Past Perfect Continuous.

WEDNESDAY | **JUN 21**

Good and *bad* MOMENTS

Yesterday started badly. I arrived at school wet and angry. I [1] _had been walking_ (walk) along the street when a car passed me. It [2] _____ (rain) and there was water everywhere. The driver went fast, right through the water which went all over me. I shouted but he [3] _____ (already / disappear) around a corner.
Then things got better. I was sitting in the lunch room looking miserable.
I [4] _____ (forget) my sandwiches and I was hungry. Suddenly, a girl came up to me and offered me some of her lunch. She [5] _____ (watch) me for a few minutes and knew what [6] _____ (happen) because she [7] _____ (notice) that every time someone got their lunch box out, I looked more and more unhappy.
Tomorrow, I'm going to take some lunch for her!

3 ** Choose the correct words.

Once, when I was on holiday, I ¹*was breaking/broke/used to break* my arm. I wasn't allowed in the sea so I ²*had sat/sat/was sitting* on the beach while all my friends ³*had swum/would swim/were swimming*. A woman with two children ⁴*came/was coming/had come* up to me and asked me if I wanted to join them looking for shells. I ⁵*hadn't been realising/hadn't realised/wouldn't realise* how many beautiful shells there were on the beach. By the end of the day, I ⁶*had been collecting/was collecting/had collected* a big bagful.

After that, shells became my passion. I ⁷*used to spend/had spent/was spending* all my time looking for shells. I ⁸*had taken/would take/had been taking* them home at the end of each holiday and put them into a big glass bowl in my room. After my mum ⁹*had washed/was washing/had been washing* them, of course!

I've still got them and I'll never forget the kind woman and her family who ¹⁰*used to make/had made/made* me happy that day.

4 *** Complete the second sentence so that it has a similar meaning to the first. Use the word in capitals.

1 I didn't think about other people when I was young.
(USE)
I *didn't use to think about other people when* I was young.

2 They would give warm tea to people queuing outside the concert hall in winter.
(USED)
They _____
outside the concert hall in winter.

3 I did my homework and then went to the cinema.
(HAD)
I went _____
my homework.

4 Mrs Davies retired from her job after 38 years of working there.
(BEEN)
Mrs Davies _____
when she retired from her job.

5 My mum often brought homeless dogs back to our house for food.
(TO)
My mum _____
homeless dogs back to our house for food.

6 My dad would never stop to give people a ride in the car.
(STOPPED)
My dad _____
a ride in the car.

Grammar Alive Telling stories

5 *** Complete the story using the cues in brackets.

1 Last Saturday, my _brother was walking home_ (brother / walk) from the shops when _he saw_ (he / see) an old lady. _She was standing_ (She / stand) by the side of a busy road.

2 _____ (He / go) into a shop for a magazine and when _____ (he / come) out, _____ (the old lady / be / still) there. _____ (She / not / move).

3 _____ (He / walk) over to her. _____ (He / not / say) anything to her, _____ (he just / step) into the road and _____ (stop) the traffic. When _____ (the cars / stop), _____ (he / take) the woman's arm and, together _____ (they / walk) to the other side.

4 Suddenly, _____ (the woman / start) shouting. _____ (She / try) to say something while _____ (they / cross) the road but _____ (my brother / not hear) her.

5 'What are you doing?' she said.
'_____ (I / not want) to cross the road. _____ (I / wait) for my bus.'

6 At that moment a bus arrived but, by the time _____ (my brother / help) the old lady back across the road, it was too late. _____ (The bus / go).

Reading

1 Read the text quickly and decide what it is about.

A A campaign for free school buses for African American schoolchildren.

B A campaign to allow children of different races to use the same school buses.

C A campaign to change the law regarding which schools children can go to.

In 1950, Linda Brown was seven years old. To get to school, she had a long, dangerous walk of over one kilometre to a bus stop. There, she had to wait for the bus to take her the rest of the way. That's not too surprising as lots of children have to travel to school by bus. What was surprising was that there was another school much nearer to her home which she wanted to go to but couldn't. Why was that?

The problem was that, as an African American, Linda Brown wasn't allowed to attend the school near to her home as it was for white children only. It sounds unbelievable today but in the 1950s children of different races were still forced to go to different schools in the USA.

At that time, the NAACP, the National Association for the Advancement of Coloured People, was trying to get equal rights for all citizens of the USA. Its members campaigned bravely, despite threats of violence. They contacted Linda's family and twelve other families in the town of Topeka, Kansas, and asked them to speak out. The families put their children's names down for the all-white school they lived near to. The NAACP knew that the school would refuse to take the children. When it did, the association took action. Its first battle was at state level but the courts in Kansas rejected their complaints. Like many people all over the USA at the time, the courts saw nothing wrong with having different schools for different races.

The NAACP didn't give up, though. It next went to the Supreme Court in Washington. The decision by the Supreme Court took a long time but, finally, on May 17th 1954, it said that it was wrong to educate children of different races in different schools. The boards of education had tried to show that all schools were equal but, in fact, in white schools $150 was spent on each student. Black schools only had $50 for each student.

Linda herself wasn't really affected by the decision. By the time the decision was made, she was in secondary school which had always taken children of different races. However, her younger sister was able to attend the mixed elementary school close to her home and didn't have to make the long journey that Linda had made every day.

Sadly, not everyone accepted the decision and there were protests. However, as attitudes slowly changed, the protests became fewer and fewer and students of all races were able to learn together.

2 Read the text again. Which of these sentences are true (T), false (F) or is there no information (NI)?

1 Linda had to wait a long time for her bus every day. _NI_

2 Linda went to the closest school to her home. ___

3 The all-white school didn't have any free places left. ___

4 The NAACP thought the all-white school would agree to take Linda. ___

5 People in Kansas held similar views on race to people in other areas of the USA. ___

6 Kansas wasn't the only state in which black children were complaining about their education. ___

7 The decision affected Linda's sister more than Linda herself. ___

8 Everyone was happy with the Supreme Court's decision. ___

3 Complete the gaps with words from the text which show the writer's opinion.

1 The walk to the bus stop: d_____

2 The fact that African American children couldn't go to school with white children in 1950: u_____

3 How the NAACP fought for equal rights: b_____

4 The fact that the decision of the Supreme Court didn't end the problem: s_____

Word Builder Multi-part verbs (2)

4 Complete the sentences with the verbs below in the correct form.

> bring forward   give up   look back on
> ~~put down~~   speak out   throw off

1 Why didn't the police _put down_ the racist protests against mixed schools?

2 The judge has decided to _____ the decision from Friday to Thursday.

3 No one _____ me _____ the bus but they did ask me to sit at the back.

4 Don't _____ your fight for equal rights.

5 When I _____ the protest march, I remember how exciting it all seemed.

6 We knew it would cause problems but we had to _____ against the unfair laws of the time.

Sentence Builder as

5 Replace the words and phrases in brackets with *as* or a phrase using *as*.

1 _As_ (Being) an African American in the 1950s, she wasn't able to do things that her white neighbours could do.

2 There were problems in many other states, _____ (for example) Mississippi, Alabama and Arkansas.

3 _____ (When) the first buses set out for the new, mixed schools, the parents anxiously watched their children leave.

4 _____ (In addition to) protests, there were attacks on some African American school children.

5 The other children are not _____ (equally famous as) Linda Brown.

6 She had to go to a school far away _____ (because) she wasn't allowed to go to her local school.

6 Make sentences from the cues using *as*.

1 / I got on / bus / realised / left / school bag / home
   As I got on the bus, I realised I had left my
   school bag at home.

2 / well / marching / we / organised / petition
   _____
   _____

3 / student / I care / education
   _____
   _____

4 I support / lot / campaigns / better education / women's rights
   _____
   _____
   _____

5 Our new campaign / not / popular / some of our other campaigns
   _____
   _____
   _____

6 I / not go / on / demonstration last weekend / had / bad cold
   _____
   _____

Listening

1 **1.12** Listen to five people talking. Match the speakers (1-5) with the opinions (a-f). There is one extra opinion.

Speaker 1 ___c___

Speaker 2 _____

Speaker 3 _____

Speaker 4 _____

Speaker 5 _____

a Animals don't have to live in the wild to be happy.

b It is dangerous to reintroduce animals to places they used to live in.

c Scientists should discover a new way to test drugs.

d There should be greater punishments for cruelty to animals.

e There are sometimes good reasons for killing animals.

f It should be more difficult to own pets.

Sentence Builder Emphasis (1)

2 **Put the words in the correct order to complete the sentences with emphasis.**

1 I dislike people who have big dogs but don't give them enough exercise.

_____*The people I dislike are those*_____

(I / those / dislike / people / the / are) who have big dogs but don't give them enough exercise.

2 I don't understand why there can't be a law against selling cosmetics that are tested on animals.

_____

(I / thing / understand / the / is / don't) why there can't be a law against selling cosmetics that are tested on animals.

3 I feel sorry for the animals which are given too much food and become very fat.

_____

(the / for / I / feel / are / ones / sorry / animals / the) which are given too much food and become very fat.

4 We support all organisations which help animals and other wildlife.

_____

(are / that / organisations / the / support / we / those) which help animals and other wildlife.

5 I admire people who spend their lives fighting for a better life for everyone.

_____

(the / people / ones / are / admire / the / I) who spend their lives fighting for a better life for everyone.

Speaking

1 **Match the beginnings (1-8) with the correct endings (a-h).**

1 Frankly, _g_

2 It's clear ___

3 It's definitely ___

4 I'm afraid I don't ___

5 That's a valid ___

6 There's no ___

7 I'm afraid I'm not ___

8 I wouldn't ___

a true that attitudes have changed a lot in the last fifty years.

b say it was a waste of time.

c point.

d that the government isn't listening to us.

e doubt that someone needs to speak out.

f convinced.

g I think demonstrations are a waste of time.

h agree with your campaign.

2 **Complete the dialogues with the words in capitals in the correct gaps. There is one extra word for each dialogue.**

1 AFRAID / ~~DOUBT~~ / FACT / FRANKLY / SURELY

A: There's no [1]____*doubt*____ that hunting is necessary.

B: I'm [2]_____ I don't agree with that at all. In [3]_____ , I think hunting is always wrong.

A: [4]_____ you can understand the need to control the number of animals if they haven't got enough to eat?

2 AGREE / CLEAR / OPINION / THINK

A: In my [5]_____ , using animals in the circus should be stopped.

B: I [6]_____ so too but it won't be easy to change people's minds in some countries.

A: I know. What is [7]_____ is that the UN should do something.

3 CONVINCED / PERSONALLY / SO / VALID / WOULDN'T

A: [8]_____ , I like the idea of bringing wolves back to Scotland.

B: I'm afraid I'm not [9]_____ . What about the sheep? They'd be eaten!

A: I [10]_____ say that. Farmers would just build bigger fences. Don't you think [11]_____ ?

8
GRAMMAR
Linking prepositions

① * **Choose the correct phrases.**

1 You should worry about your school work *as a result of/instead of* worrying about your weight.

2 We can never be sure that photos are 'real' *because of/in spite of* Photoshop and similar computer programmes.

3 I'd never have cosmetic surgery *in spite of/instead of* all the magazine articles I have read about how good it can make you feel.

4 *In addition to/Except for* a nose job, my friend also wants to make her lips bigger.

5 Some adverts have been banned *apart from/as a result of* pressure from angry parents.

6 *Except for/Instead of* one aunt, I don't know anyone who has had cosmetic surgery.

7 *In spite of/Apart from* making you feel bad about yourself, magazines also make you judge other people.

② ** **Complete the text with the words below. Two phrases can go in the same gap.**

apart from   ~~because of~~   except for
in addition to   in spite of   instead of

The National Advertising Division (NAD) in the USA has changed the laws on advertising ¹ _because of_ a magazine advert that used Photoshop. The photo showed what would happen if you used a certain cosmetic. However, the picture had been Photoshopped. ² _____ a small message at the bottom of the advert to say the photo had been changed, the NAD said that this was unacceptable.

The question now is, what other things will be affected? ³ _____/_____ cosmetics, other products are also shown to be better than they really are. Think back to when you were last in a fast-food restaurant. ⁴ _____ the beautiful, juicy burger with fresh lettuce and tomato in the posters, I'm sure what you got was a dried-up piece of meat with a sad-looking piece of lettuce on it. No one believes the pictures they see in such restaurants, ⁵ _____ those few people who have never eaten fast food before, so does it matter?

③ ** **Choose the correct answers.**

1 _a_ Photoshop, I know two other good photo-editing programmes.
   a Apart from   **b** Instead of   **c** Because of

2 ____ complaining about these photos, why don't you just enjoy the artistic results of the computer programme.
   a Because of   **b** In addition to   **c** Instead of

3 ____ giving you a beautiful tan, this cream can also hide your wrinkles.
   a In spite of   **b** Except for   **c** In addition to

4 ____ complaints from readers, the magazine has stopped using Photoshop.
   a Instead of   **b** Because of   **c** In spite of

5 ____ reading all these fashion magazines, my daughter has decided to become a photographer.
   a Instead of   **b** Except for   **c** As a result of

6 ____ all the beauty tips and diet plans, people don't look much different to how they looked twenty years ago.
   a As a result of   **b** In spite of   **c** Apart from

④ *** **Complete the second sentence so that it has the same meaning as the first. Use the word in capitals.**

1 We picked up the litter and we washed the graffiti off the walls.
   (ADDITION)
   _____*In addition to picking up the litter*_____ , we washed the graffiti off the walls.

2 Due to our efforts, our town received a 'clean city' award.
   (RESULT)
   _____ , our town received a 'clean city' award.

3 200 people turned up to help although the weather was awful.
   (SPITE)
   _____ , 200 people turned up to help.

4 The only people there were school students.
   (FROM)
   _____ , there was no one there.

5 Don't sit there complaining, do something to help!
   (INSTEAD)
   _____ , do something to help.

6 The only person who didn't join the protest was Tom, who is in hospital.
   (FOR)
   Everyone joined the protest _____ , who is in hospital.

Writing Workshop 2

1 Look at the opinion essay. Label the paragraphs (A-D) with the headings below. Then put the paragraphs in the correct order.

Main point
Conclusion
Introduction
Opposing point of view

Organic food is better than non-organic food

A _____

[1](On the other hand)/ In addition, some people have pointed out the negative aspects of organic food production. Farms using organic farming methods produce less food than traditional farms. [2]As a result/For instance, organic farms mean that we need to use more land for farming.

B _Introduction_ _1_

We have been using the term 'organic farming' for over 70 years but what does it really mean? On organic farms, chemicals can't be used on plants or fed to animals. As people worry about the effect of these chemicals, organic food is becoming more and more popular.

C _____

[3]Moreover/To sum up, [4]however/despite the lack of scientific evidence to say that organic food is healthier than non-organic food, [5]in my opinion/ according to me it is better to be careful about what we put in the ground and feed to our animals. If scientists do find some problems in the future, it might be too late to do anything about them.

D _____

[6]As well/According to many people, organic food is healthier and tastier than other food. [7]Furthermore/ Apart from, organic farming is less harmful to the environment. [8]As well as/However leading to less pollution, organic farming usually uses less energy. [9]Despite/Moreover, organic farms are able to recycle more of the waste they produce as the waste is more natural and less contaminated.

2 Read the text again and choose the correct words (1-9).

3 Complete the second sentence so that it has the same meaning as the first. Use the word in capitals.

1 There are several small shops in our village which may close down, such as the local butchers. (FOR)
There are several shops in our village which may close down, _for instance_ the local butchers.

2 In conclusion, I believe that the freshness of the food is worth the small extra cost. (UP)
_____ ,
I believe that the freshness of the food is worth the small extra cost.

3 I don't go shopping very often but I always use the local shops when I can. (DESPITE)
_____
very often, I always use the local shops when I can.

4 I think that the food in local shops is fresher than the food in supermarkets. (OPINION)
_____
the food in local shops is fresher than the food in supermarkets.

5 Experts say that supermarkets are so popular because of the free parking. (ACCORDING)
_____
supermarkets are so popular because of the free parking.

6 My parents only go to the supermarket for tinned food and things like pasta and flour. (FROM)
_____
tinned food and things like pasta and flour, my parents don't buy anything in the supermarket.

7 However, I can understand why people who don't have much time or money prefer shopping at supermarkets. (HAND)
_____ ,
I can understand why people who don't have much time or money prefer shopping at supermarkets.

4 Read the instructions below and write an opinion essay on the topic. Use the ideas from Exercise 3 if you want to.

Buying food in smaller shops is better than in large supermarkets.
- Introduce the essay.
- Discuss some reasons why small shops are better places to shop than supermarkets.
- Give some reasons why some people prefer shopping in supermarkets.
- Conclude the essay giving your opinions and reasons for them.

Write between 120 and 180 words.

Check Your Progress 2

1 Campaigns Complete the words with one word in each gap.

We're campaigning for:

1 wildlife c_____ .   2 freedom of s_____ .

We're campaigning against:

3 nuclear p_____ .   4 animal t_____ .

We're going to:

5 d_____ money.   6 s_____ a petition.

/6

2 Talking about the past and Past Perfect Continuous Choose the correct forms.

1 I *used to/did/would* love eating meat but now I'm a vegetarian.

2 When I worked at the help centre, we *had spent/ have been spending/would spend* ages every evening talking to lonely people on the phone.

3 I *wouldn't know/hadn't known/wasn't knowing* how many people were homeless until my uncle took me to the soup kitchen.

4 They *would collect/used to collect/had been collecting* money all morning and they had £1000.

5 We *did/had done/were doing* our shopping when the old man stopped us.

/5

3 Multi-part verbs (2) Complete the sentences with one word in each gap.

1 A boy was _____ off the train today because he didn't have a ticket.

2 The government hasn't got enough soldiers to put _____ our movement.

3 Why did you _____ up your seat to that man? You needed it more than he did.

4 Don't be scared to say what you think. We should all speak _____ about unfairness in society.

5 It's good to look _____ on things that you did when you were younger.

/5

4 as Complete the sentences with as or a phrase using as.

1 We're organising a march _____ a petition.

2 Many famous people support us, _____ Sir Paul McCartney and JK Rowling.

3 This march isn't _____ big _____ last year's.

4 The demonstration wasn't shown on television _____ the police stopped photographers entering the area.

5 Emphasis (1) Complete the second sentence so that it has the same meaning as the first.

1 I support Greenpeace.
The organisation _____

2 I don't understand people who won't try organic food.
The people I _____

3 I hate people who drive too fast.
The people I _____

4 I worry about the health service.
The thing _____

5 I like our farm shop because of the fresh fruit.
The thing I like about _____

/5

6 Linking prepositions Complete the sentences with the words below. There is one extra word.

apart   except   in spite   instead
as a result   in addition

1 _____ of worrying about the environment, do something about it.

2 _____ of the rain, not many people went on the march.

3 _____ of our protests, the government refuses to change its mind about education.

4 _____ to working as a volunteer, I also take part in fundraising activities.

5 _____ for Sally, the only person who stayed behind to help clear up was me.

/5

TOTAL SCORE **/30**

Module Diary

1 Look at the objectives on page 15 in the Students' Book. Choose three and evaluate your learning.

1 Now I can _____
well / quite well / with problems.

2 Now I can _____
well / quite well / with problems.

3 Now I can _____
well / quite well / with problems.

2 Look at your results. What language areas in this module do you need to study more?

/4

Exam Choice 1

Reading

1 **Read the text quickly and choose the best title.**

A The rise and fall of the supermarkets
B A history of campaigns against supermarkets
C Our changing shopping habits

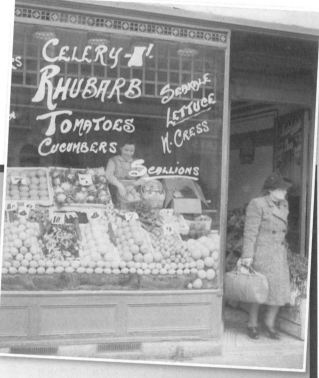

In 1947, there were just ten self-service shops in the whole of the UK. Shops often sold just one type of product, for instance just meat or fruit and vegetables. Others sold a variety of food but, instead of the customer collecting the items they wanted, they sat in a chair near the counter while the shop assistant collected everything for them.

Supermarkets had already taken off in the USA, though, and, in 1940, 40 percent of all food there was sold in self-service shops. As people started earning more money after the war and different kinds of food became available, supermarkets came to the UK, too.

Slowly, they took over. As they opened more and more stores, the supermarkets were able to offer lower prices. Not only that, they were often large enough to have their own car parks where customers could park for free, unlike town centre shops whose customers had to pay to park or use the bus. Larger and larger stores opened but often outside the town centres. In addition to offering food, they also started selling clothes, toys, cosmetics and other things. People no longer needed to go to the town centre at all. Even those who preferred to buy their meat or bread locally soon decided that it wasn't worth making an extra trip just for these few items. It was easier to buy them in the supermarket, too.

Although many people were happy with the cheap food and the ease of doing all their shopping in one place, others were less pleased. They were upset that their town centres were now full of closed-up shops with nowhere to buy fresh food anymore. This unhappiness led to campaigns and protests. Most of these were local, trying to stop a supermarket opening in a particular town.

These campaign groups have several reasons for their protests. They represent farmers who are forced to sell their food to supermarkets very cheaply. They represent shop workers who are often paid very poorly. They also care about the environment. Food sold in supermarkets has often travelled thousands of miles to get to the shop. Smaller shops sell much more locally produced food which doesn't need planes and lorries to transport it.

These protests do seem to be working. The local food movement is growing all over the world and many towns have seen markets and farm shops opening up. Supermarkets aren't about to disappear but customers have shown that they want more choice than even these giant shops can offer.

2 Read the text again. Which of these sentences are true (T), false (F) or is there no information (NI)?

1 The first self-service shops in Britain opened in 1947.
____

2 Supermarkets were already popular in the USA before 1947.
____

3 One reason why supermarkets came to the UK was because people had more money to spend.
____

4 One reason why early supermarkets were popular was because they offered free buses.
____

5 People stopped buying meat and bread from local shops because they preferred the food in the supermarket.
____

6 Not everyone is unhappy with supermarkets.
____

7 Supermarkets don't employ as many people as local shops used to.
____

8 It is now easier to buy locally produced food than it was a few years ago.
____

Listening

3 🔊1.13 Listen to five people talking. Match the speakers (1-5) with the problems (a-f). There is one extra problem.

Speaker 1 ____
Speaker 2 ____
Speaker 3 ____
Speaker 4 ____
Speaker 5 ____

a Keeping two parents happy.
b A medical emergency.
c A relationship.
d Forgetting an important occasion.
e Viewing a social network page.
f A lack of ideas.

4 🔊1.13 Listen again and choose the correct answers.

1 Emma is coming to visit her family this weekend because:
a they are having a party.
b someone is ill.
c she wants to say sorry to her parents.

2 The mother didn't want her ex-husband to:
a come to her birthday party.
b see photos of her birthday party.
c be a Facebook friend of her son.

3 The girl is worried because:
a her father might not like her boyfriend.
b one parent will be upset whatever she decides to do.
c she doesn't get on with her father's new family.

4 The boy was upset because his girlfriend didn't:
a want to visit him in hospital.
b like the meal he paid for.
c want him to eat something he liked.

5 The boy would like to:
a write a blog.
b start up a campaign.
c have more Facebook friends.

Speaking

5 Complete the dialogue with the words below.

afraid agree clear convinced
opinion personally sorry true

Angie: In my ¹_____ , families are more important than friends. ²_____ , I am closer to my mother and sister than to anyone at school. I don't think you can really ever trust a friend.

Jo: I'm ³_____ I don't ⁴_____ with you at all. When you say families are important, I think you are right but, I'm ⁵_____ , it's just not ⁶_____ that you can never trust a friend. What's ⁷_____ to me is that you haven't met a real friend yet. When you do, you won't feel like you feel now.

Angie: I'm not ⁸_____ . I don't think I'll ever meet such a person.

Exam Choice 1

Use of English

6 Complete the text with one word in each gap.

When I was a child, life was very uncomplicated. My parents made all my decisions for me except ¹_____ which toys I was going to play with! I used ²_____ get pocket money but it was ³_____ little that, by the time I ⁴_____ bought a few sweets on a Saturday morning, there was almost nothing left. ⁵_____ a result, I didn't have to worry about what to spend my money on or whether I should save it.

Now I'm 16 years old and I have quite a lot ⁶_____ freedom and responsibility in my life. My parents give me money but it is for clothes, going out and things I need for school. It's ⁷_____ to me what I spend it on but, when it's gone I can't get anymore until the beginning of the next month. Apart ⁸_____ financial decisions, I am also responsible for planning my work time and what to do when I'm not working. My parents trust me not to waste my time on computer games when I should be studying.

Hardly ⁹_____ of my friends have so much freedom and they think it is quite strange but I think it is a great idea. I've made a ¹⁰_____ mistakes but not many and none of them have ¹¹_____ very serious. We learn from our mistakes so, when I leave home and go to university, it will be easier for me to make important decisions.

Writing

7 Match the beginnings (1-6) with the correct endings (a-f).

1 To be _____
2 As you _____
3 In _____
4 According _____
5 By the _____
6 It'll be fun, especially _____

a fact, climate change is a better phrase than global warming.

b way, if you decide to come, you'll need some food and drink.

c honest, I'd never worried about climate change before.

d to my dad, the winters were wetter than they are now.

e if Debbie and her friend Hannah decide to join us.

f know, we've had some strange weather recently.

8 Read the instructions below and write an email to a friend. Use the ideas in Exercise 7 if you want to.

- Explain why you are interested in climate change.
- Invite your friend to a protest march you are going on.
- Give extra information about what to bring on the march.

Write between 120 and 180 words.

TOPIC TALK – VOCABULARY

1 **Match the headlines (1-7) with the correct types of print media (a-g).**

1 Summer dresses from new Italian designer _d_

2 **Guitarist, Benji, to form a new band** ___

3 Inside – an interview with Oscar-winning director, Dan Hart ___

4 **Elections in Peru – what do the results mean?** ___

5 **New car park to open in the town centre** ___

6 **112 great pages Every Saturday Only £1.20** ___

7 Is your husband telling you the truth? ___

a local newspaper
b women's magazine
c news and current affairs magazine
d fashion magazine
e weekly magazine
f music magazine
g film magazine

2 **Choose the correct answers.**

1 He has some great guests.
  a chat show   **b** documentary   **c** soap opera

2 It is always really funny.
  a sitcom   **b** documentary   **c** drama series

3 Last week's report on homelessness was really interesting.
  a documentary   **b** reality show   **c** chat show

4 You can win a million pounds by answering ten questions.
  a discussion   **b** game show   **c** soap opera

5 There are ten people who have to show how good they are in business. Each week, one person gets thrown off. The winner gets money and a job.
  a reality show   **b** documentary   **c** sitcom

6 This story about a street in northern England has been on TV for fifty years - and actor William Roache has been in it since the start.
  a reality show   **b** soap opera   **c** the news

7 It's useful to know if it is going to rain tomorrow.
  a drama series   **b** documentary
  c the weather forecast

8 Some people who ring the programme are quite strange.
  a play   **b** sitcom
  c phone-in programme

3 **Complete the sentences with one word in each gap.**

1 This c_celebrity___ website is full of photos and Hollywood gossip.

2 This is a f_____-s _____ website but they make sure that there's nothing illegal on it.

3 H_____ websites can be useful but doctors are better.

4 Why does anyone pay £3.99 for a magazine when the o_____ version is free?

5 Our s_____ website is brilliant. There are photos from sports days, timetables, information about the teachers and holiday dates.

6 I use two main r_____ websites. One is a dictionary and the other is an encyclopedia.

7 There are other s_____ e_____ apart from Google but they don't give you so many results.

8 I've uploaded three of my films to v_____-s_____ websites. I'm hoping a Hollywood director will see them!

9 My favourite comedian has a free p_____ every week which I always download and listen to on my MP3 player.

4 **Complete the text with the words below.**

blog catch check chill comments discussions encyclopedias listen networking ~~read~~ watch

I ¹ _read___ a newspaper everyday because I'm very interested in current affairs. I also ² _____ the news on TV and ³ _____ to the radio when I'm having my breakfast. I ⁴ _____ out the latest news on the internet as well because I'm worried I'll miss something important.

To ⁵ _____ out, I listen to online radio or watch television. My favourite programmes are ⁶ _____ but I also watch documentaries and one or two sitcoms.

When I want to express my opinions, I write a ⁷ _____ or I post ⁸ _____ on different websites. When I am doing research for school, I use online ⁹ _____ but I always check the facts on two or three sites because they aren't always accurate.

To ¹⁰ _____ up on my friends' news, I look at their social ¹¹ _____ pages. All my friends have got them so it's easy to waste a lot of time looking at them.

SKILLS
Reading

1 Read the two texts quickly and decide which is factual (F) and which is unreliable and biased (U). Then complete the words in the phrases from the texts (1-6).

Text A _____

1 Daytime temperatures are e_xpected__ to reach ...

2 The g_____ has w_____ drivers ...

3 ... weather o_____ are h_____ that ...

Text B _____

4 ... as people in Crawley, West Sussex s_____ into work ...

5 A_____ , the workers in the town ...

6 They've p_____ been told...

A

BREAKING NEWS

Weather

Feb 1st

The government put out a level three warning today as temperatures in the country dropped to -9°C. There are four levels of warning, a level four is the most dangerous. Heavy snow has caused chaos on the roads. ⁱ _d_ Daytime temperatures are expected to reach 1°C tomorrow with further snow and ice forecast. The government has warned drivers to be extra careful and only to travel if necessary. ⁱⁱ___ Many trains are not running and airports have closed because of snow and freezing fog.

Comments: What's wrong with this country? -9°C! It's not the end of the world, is it? It's -30°C in Eastern Europe. That's cold!

The problem is that we're not used to snow. People don't have winter tyres on their cars. That's why there are so many accidents.

Feb 3rd

Temperatures fell to -11°C in many areas. More snow is expected today. ⁱⁱⁱ___

Feb 7th

The UK seems to have dodged the bullet as the cold spell at last begins to run out of steam. Temperatures are still cold but skies are clear and the warm sun has started to melt the snow. The A1 road which was blocked for 40 km because of 43 accidents caused by ice has now reopened. The government is warning drivers to be careful. ^{iv}___ In fact, it can mean the opposite. Roads are now wet because of the melting snow and this could turn into black ice overnight.

Feb 11th

Temperatures in the UK fell to -18°C last night, colder than in Moscow. However, weather officials are hopeful that this could be the end of the cold spell. ^v___

B

Why can't we cope with the weather?

Did you know that on February 15th, as people in Crawley, West Sussex struggled into work by car or train, their bins remained unemptied. ^{vi}_____ Apparently, the workers in the town who usually empty the bins are 'afraid of slipping on the ice'. They've probably been told by their health and safety officers that it's too dangerous.

Comments: The dustmen used to collect the rubbish in all kinds of weather. What's happened to people nowadays?

What are you all moaning about? On February 23rd a sudden change in wind direction took temperatures from record lows to record highs in just a few days. In the east of England, temperatures rose to 18°C, warmer than some parts of North Africa. Beaches where I live were full of families with children enjoying a very unusual half term break. Now that the cold weather has gone, though, the experts can't relax and enjoy themselves. Oh no, they have to start worrying about the next problem. ^{vii}_____ Water companies are now warning that there won't be enough water this summer and that we can expect a drought.

Comments: We should get used to this strange weather. Climate change doesn't just mean warmer temperatures. It means more extreme weather of all kinds.

2 **Read the text again. Match the sentences (a–h) with the gaps in the texts (i–vii). There is one extra sentence.**

a This could turn to ice as temperatures again fall to under zero tonight.

b This is because a change in wind direction should bring warmer temperatures soon.

c Despite the snow, it has been a very dry winter.

d Many of them are blocked because of accidents.

e They enjoyed the snow and played on sledges or made snowmen.

f The warm sun does not mean that the roads are safe.

g There are also problems with other forms of transport.

h The collection of rubbish from outside people's houses just stopped.

Word Builder Idiomatic language (1)

3 **Complete the sentences with one word.**

1 When you are worried about something and the danger passes, you may breathe a sigh of
relief .

2 When a person or place has a lucky escape, we can say that they dodged the _____ .

3 The worst thing people can do in a crisis is to lose their _____ . They should try to stay calm and not panic.

4 Sometimes people get depressed over small problems. You may try to cheer them up by telling them not to worry because it isn't the end of the
_____ .

5 When you think other people are making a problem bigger than it really is you can tell them that it isn't a big problem at all. It's just a storm in a
_____ .

6 When someone or something starts to slow down or fade away, you can say that the person or thing is running out of _____ .

4 **Complete the sentences with the idiomatic phrases from Exercise 3 in the correct form.**

1 I don't know why people _lose their heads_ and start to scream when they see famous pop stars or film stars.

2 Come on, it's only a football match. It isn't
_____ . Maybe we'll win next week.

3 I _____ when I found that I hadn't lost my phone.

4 I started a blog a month ago full of enthusiasm but I soon _____ and have now stopped writing completely.

5 The argument with Sara is just a
_____ . She'll forget all about it in a day or two.

6 A lot of people at school got into trouble because of what they wrote in their blogs. I
_____ because I managed to remove mine before anyone saw it.

Sentence Builder used to

5 **Complete the sentences with the correct form of the verbs in brackets.**

1 I didn't use _to watch_ (watch) the news on TV but now I never miss it.

2 The UK isn't used _____ (have) lots of snow.

3 When you're a celebrity, you get used _____ (see) your name in the newspapers.

4 I used _____ (love) snow when I was younger.

5 We've got used _____ (read) about extreme weather events recently.

6 Did you use _____ (go) skiing when you were young?

7 Are you used _____ (live) in a country which has real, cold winters?

8 How long did it take you to get used _____ (be) a celebrity?

10

GRAMMAR
Verb patterns

Complete Exercises A-B before you start this lesson.

A Match the beginnings (1-9) with the correct endings (a-c) for each group of sentences.

1 My mum made me __c__   **a** brushing my hair.
2 My little sister likes ___   **b** to brush my hair.
3 I refused ___   **c** brush my hair.

4 My dad agreed ___   **a** drive the car.
5 She loves ___   **b** to drive the car.
6 He let us ___   **c** driving the car.

7 My brother helped ___   **a** doing my homework.
8 I admitted ___   **b** not doing my homework.
9 I can't stand ___   **c** me to do my homework.

B Complete the sentences with the correct form of the verbs in brackets.

1 The police won't let us ___march___ (march).
2 My mum asked me _____ (help) her with the computer.
3 I admitted _____ (break) the window.
4 We refused _____ (work) after 5 p.m.
5 My mum made me _____ (learn) French.
6 I can't stand _____ (wait) for a bus.
7 Did you manage _____ (find) your wallet?
8 My brother always avoids _____ (do) the washing-up.

❶ * Choose the correct verb form.

1 I avoid *to watch*/*watching* reality shows.
2 I've managed *to upload*/*uploading* our film to YouTube.
3 I don't mind *to wait*/*waiting*. I've got lots to read.
4 I've decided *to become*/*becoming* a journalist.
5 Have you finished *to read*/*reading* the newspaper?
6 I don't want *to watch*/*watching* this programme.
7 It's worth *to download*/*downloading* these podcasts. They're excellent.
8 Do you really enjoy *to work*/*working* here?
9 I prefer *to write*/*writing* blogs to reading them.
10 I'm not used *to get*/*to getting* up early in the morning.

❷ ** Complete the text with the correct form of the verbs below.

~~buy~~ do find not finish read (x 4) spend switch

My parents always used ¹ ___to buy___ a newspaper from the local shop but they never managed ² _____ all the articles. They didn't mind ³ _____ it because it was cheap. Now, though, they don't have so much money and my dad says it isn't worth ⁴ _____ £1 every day on a newspaper when you can read it online for nothing. He used ⁵ _____ the paper on the train to work but now he's retired. He still enjoys ⁶ _____ out what's happening in the world but he prefers ⁷ _____ it online.

My mum can't stand ⁸ _____ things online so she's given up ⁹ _____ the paper completely. She listens to the radio in the kitchen where she spends most of her time. Well, she listens to it when she remembers ¹⁰ _____ it on.

❸ ** Make sentences from the cues (a-f) and match them with the correct pictures (1-6).

a Try / finish / before midnight
Try to finish before midnight.

b Please / stop / shout!
_____

c Do you regret / come / here / for your holiday?
_____

d Can we stop / take photo?
_____

e Try / tidy / your desk
_____

f I remember / watch / first episode / this soap opera
_____

4 *** Complete the dialogues with the correct form of the verbs below.

> forget / send   regret / say   remember / read
> stop / watch   ~~try / download~~

1 a A: I can't listen to this online radio show.
> B: *Try downloading* it first. It might work then.
> b A: What's wrong?
> B: I _____ a film and it made my computer crash.

2 a A: The USA has been hit by a hurricane.
> B: Oh yes. I _____ about that when it was over Cuba.
> b A: Did you _____ that article I told you about?
> B: Yes, but I didn't understand it.

3 a A: I haven't got any time for my homework.
> B: Well, _____ reality shows then.
> b A: Why aren't you doing your homework?
> B: I _____ the weather forecast for tomorrow.

4 a A: Have you read the newspaper today?
> B: I _____ that I haven't.

4 b A: You told Mrs Clark that a hurricane was coming. She said she was really worried.
> B: I know. I _____ that now but I thought it was true at the time.

5 a A: What do you remember about the start of your writing career?
> B: Well, I'll never _____ my first article to a newspaper.

5 b A: See you in two weeks.
> B: Have a good time. Don't _____ me a postcard.

Grammar Alive
Telling people what to do

5 *** Make sentences from the cues.

Lisa spends all her time watching reality shows.

1 **Sister:** stop / watch that rubbish!
> *Stop watching that rubbish!*
> _____

2 **Dad:** you / regret / waste / your time / when / you have exams
> _____
> _____

3 **Mum:** don't forget / do / homework
> _____
> _____

4 **Brother:** remember / switch off / television / when / go / bed
> _____
> _____

Emily left school at sixteen with no qualifications

5 **Dad:** you / regret / not / get / any qualifications / if / can't find / job
> _____
> _____

6 **Friend:** why don't / try / go / evening classes?
> _____
> _____

7 **Mum:** don't forget / clean / fingernails / before / go for / your job interview
> _____
> _____

8 **Teacher:** I / regret / say that / won't be easy / find a good job
> _____
> _____

11 SKILLS
Oral Skills

Listening

NEW YORK HERALD

THE WILD ANIMALS BROKEN LOOSE FROM CENTRAL PARK!!

SAVAGE BRUTES AT LARGE!!!

1 🔊 **1.14 Listen to a description of a news story and choose the correct answers.**

1 In 1867:
   a *The New York Herald* published a hoax story.
   b James Bennett took over *The New York Herald*.
   c *The New York Herald* financed an expedition.

2 When people realised that the story was untrue, many of them:
   a thought that James Bennett was responsible.
   b knew that it was Thomas Connery's idea.
   c blamed the writer, Joseph Clarke.

3 People could have discovered that the story was untrue if:
   a they had read the message at the end of the story.
   b they had understood the headline.
   c they had read that day's *The New York Times*.

4 When people complained about the story, *The New York Herald*:
   a apologised and promised not to write any more hoax stories.
   b sacked the writer responsible.
   c said that it had been a warning.

2 🔊 **1.14 Listen again and match the words in the listening with the correct meanings.**

1 hoax: a(n) *true/*untrue* story which intends to trick people

2 influential: *able to change the way people think/ accurate and reliable*

3 to finance: *to write about/to pay for*

4 to make up: *to use your imagination to create a story/to investigate carefully to write a story*

5 to remain: *to stay/to return*

6 to criticise: to express *approval/disapproval* of someone or something

7 panic: a sudden feeling of *fear/anger* that makes you unable to think clearly

Speaking

1 **Choose the correct words.**

1 I started my new school last September. *At first/ Firstly*, it was quite strange but I'm used to it now.

2 We were waiting for ages but *anyway/eventually* someone came to show us where to go.

3 I switched on the TV *as soon as/then* I got home.

4 It was *so/such* a good film that I bought the DVD.

5 It took a long time to finish my homework but *at first/in the end*, I was able to put my books away.

2 **Read the text and put the paragraphs (A–E) in the correct order.**

A ___
At [1] ___*first*___ , the guests didn't realise it was a spoof. It was just [2] _____ watching their facial expressions. In one show, he visited an environmental protest in London.

B ___
He finally joins the protest and, as [3] _____ as he does, he starts shouting at the police. In the [4] _____ , he runs into the street and the protesters are [5] _____ angry with his behaviour that they ask the police to arrest him!

C ___
He then suggests it would be better to knock down older cinemas and 'build trees' there instead. The [6] _____ thing that [7] _____ is that he asks a policeman who would win a fight between the police and the protesters.

D _1_
I love Sacha Baron Cohen. Now he is [8] _____ but when he first started, no one knew who he was. In his programme, *Ali G*, he interviewed people but asked them really strange questions.

E ___
The scene starts [9] _____ with him asking what the protest is about. A woman tells him that they want to stop trees being cut down and a new cinema being built.

3 🔊 **1.15 Complete the text with the words below. Then listen to check.**

end ~~first~~ happens famous hilarious
next off so soon

12 GRAMMAR Negation

LESSON

1 * Complete the sentences with one of the words in capitals.

NO / ANY

1 I haven't got ___any___ qualifications for this job.

2 He's got _____ qualifications for this job.

3 _____ reality show is worth watching.

4 There isn't _____ reality show that is worth watching.

5 They gave me _____ reason why my article wasn't published.

FEW / LITTLE

6 _____ young people buy a newspaper every day.

7 There are _____ really funny sitcoms these days.

8 _____ money is spent on new programmes.

9 I've got very _____ ideas for my blog.

10 I've got very _____ trust in anything I see advertised.

2 ** Complete the dialogues with the words in capitals. Use each word once.

~~ANY~~ / ANY / FEW / LITTLE / NO

A: Have you read [1] ___any___ articles about this year's Oscars?

B: No. [2]_____ of the films are of interest to me. I saw one of them but that's all. There's very [3]_____ chance of [4]_____ of the films I like getting an Oscar.

A: [5]_____ film that you like will ever win an Oscar. I can guarantee that!

ANY / ANY / FEW / LITTLE / NO

A: Oh no. Another reality show. Why do people want to appear on them? [6]_____ person who goes on a reality show must be mad.

B: Why? [7]_____ other programmes give normal, untalented, people a chance to become famous. You have to be able to sing or dance to win a talent show. Most people can't do those things very well and they have very [8]_____ opportunities to do well in life. Why shouldn't they try to be a reality star?

A: Because people often laugh at them.

B: But that can't be [9]_____ worse than getting very [10]_____ respect when they are unemployed or doing a boring job every day.

3 *** Rewrite the sentence using the word in capitals so that it has a similar meaning.

1 There isn't much to do here. (LITTLE)
_____There is very little to do here._____

2 I have read nothing interesting so far. (ANYTHING)
_____
_____

3 You should never believe what you read. (EVER)
_____
_____

4 There are few blogs which interest me. (MANY)
_____
_____

5 I can't do this with no help. (ANY)
_____
_____

6 There wasn't anyone funny on the show. (NO ONE)
_____
_____

7 I've got very little time to read a newspaper. (LOT)
_____
_____

8 I've seen nothing to make me change my mind about reality shows. (ANYTHING)
_____
_____

9 I haven't heard very much about the hurricane in the Atlantic. (LITTLE)
_____
_____

Sentence Builder *hardly*

4 Complete the sentences with a phrase using *hardly*.

1 Newspapers ___hardly ever___ (very rarely) apologise when they make mistakes.

2 _____ (Very few) of my friends like reality shows.

3 Real news _____ (almost doesn't get) discussed at all nowadays.

4 Mark is so lazy. He _____ (almost doesn't move) at all when we play football.

5 Chat shows _____ (don't often) have interesting guests on them.

6 My blog is great but _____ (very few) people have read it.

7 My sister _____ (almost doesn't eat) any vegetables.

8 _____ (Almost no) students in my class watch the news.

Writing Workshop 3

1 Complete the review with the words below.

scenes sum appear ~~series~~ mockumentary
however duo concept worst repetitive

Life's Too Short

I want to write about the TV
[1]____series____ *Life's Too Short*. It's a
[2]_____ about a talent agent
who is only 105 cm tall and it was written
by two comedians, Ricky Gervais and
Stephen Merchant. The [3]_____
have already made two other series
together and they also [4]_____
in this, along with Warwick Davis who
plays the lead part, and, each week, a
different, famous Hollywood star.

The [5]_____ is similar to
both their previous shows. Gervais and
Merchant play themselves and, whenever
Davis goes to see them to ask if they've
got any work for him, they are always
with one of their guests. Liam Neeson
and Johnny Depp are just two of the stars
appearing in the series. Some
[6]_____ are hilarious and
Gervais and Merchant are always funny
together.

[7]_____ , the main problem is
that we find ourselves waiting to see the
'real' stars and Warwick Davis's character
is less interesting. Also, such a lot of the
jokes involve Davis falling over that it gets
quite [8]_____ .
[9]_____ of all, there is so much
in it that is similar to *The Office* and
Extras that it seems as if the writers have
run out of ideas.

To [10]_____ up, the show has
some very funny bits but sometimes you
feel that Gervais and Merchant are doing
so many things that they haven't had time
to really concentrate on this programme.
It's good but it should be much better.

Sentence Builder Result linkers (2)

2 Make sentences from the cues.

1 I (have got / so / ideas) __*I've got so many ideas that*__
I'm writing three articles at the same time.
2 Cinema tickets (cost / so / money) _____
_____
I never buy popcorn.
3 The chat show host (have / lot / guests on his show)
_____
_____
he only had time to ask them one question each.
4 There (be / lot / rubbish on TV) _____
_____
I never watch it.
5 There (be / much / repetition) _____
_____
you know what they are going to say before they say it.

3 Match the beginnings (1-7) with the correct endings (a-g).

The Annoying Orange - The Onion Ring
1 There are lots _g_
2 There are so ___
3 Most of ___
4 The concept is ___
5 The orange has got such ___
6 However, they can get a bit ___
7 Worst of ___

a repetitive after a while.
b many of them that I don't think I've seen them all.
c similar to the horror film *The Ring*.
d all, since they became popular, the makers of the films seem to have run out of ideas.
e them are hilarious.
f an annoying laugh and tells such terrible jokes that it is called 'The Annoying Orange'.
g of funny 'Annoying Orange' videos but this is the funniest.

4 Read the instructions below and describe your favourite YouTube video.

- Say something about the video. For example, is it part of a series?
- Talk about what you like about it.
- Give any negative points.
- Sum up with your opinions.

Write between 80 and 120 words.

Check Your Progress 3

① The media Complete the words.

1 A m_____ magazine comes out 12 times a year.

2 A t_____ newspaper is smaller in size and usually has more gossip and less serious news.

3 A c_____ programme is funny.

4 A d_____ is a programme about a real subject such as education, war, history or science.

5 A r_____ website helps you to find out facts.

6 A s_____ e_____ helps you to find websites that you are interested in.

/6

② Idiomatic language (1) Complete the sentences with one word in each gap.

1 Mark b_____ a sigh of relief when he passed his driving test.

2 Some people l_____ their heads when they felt the ground shaking.

3 The storm r_____ out of steam before it hit land.

4 We d_____ the bullet yesterday but next time we may not be so lucky.

5 Stop crying. This problem of yours i_____ just a storm in a teacup. You'll soon forget it.

/5

③ *used to* Put the words in brackets into the correct form.

1 I _____ (used / have) problems sleeping at night.

2 I've _____ (get / used / go) to school by bus now.

3 I don't think I'll ever _____ (get / used / get) up so early.

4 My mum _____ (not / use / work) but now she does.

5 My dad _____ (be / used / be) a house husband now.

/5

④ Verb patterns Complete the sentences with the correct form of the verbs in brackets.

1 I tried _____ (find) a summer job.

2 Don't forget _____ (send) Tom an email.

3 I don't regret _____ (close) my social networking page. I've got lots more time now.

4 Stop _____ (talk) and listen to me!

5 I don't remember _____ (comment) on your blog. What did I write?

/5

⑤ Negation Complete the dialogue with the words below.

> any   ever   few   little   no

A: There are [1]_____ films on TV tonight.

B: Well, the films on TV are hardly [2]_____ worth watching. Very [3]_____ people I know watch films on television now. They prefer DVDs or download films from the internet so that they don't have to watch the adverts.

A: That's because you and your friends like strange films. I can usually find one I like but there aren't [4]_____ at all tonight. Not even a late-night horror film. Doesn't it annoy you?

B: Not really. I've got very [5]_____ time to watch films at the moment because of my exams but, if there's nothing you want to watch, I'll have a break from my studies and watch the news.

/5

⑥ Result linkers (2) Rewrite the sentence beginnings using the words in capitals.

1 There are such a lot of famous people here that …
(SO) _____

2 There is so much to do here that …
(SUCH)_____

3 There are so many interesting programmes on television tonight that …
(SUCH)_____

4 They gave me such a lot of information that …
(SO) _____

/4

TOTAL SCORE */30*

Module Diary

① Look at the objectives on page 25 in the Students' Book. Choose three and evaluate your learning.

1 Now I can _____
well / quite well / with problems.

2 Now I can _____
well / quite well / with problems.

3 Now I can _____
well / quite well / with problems.

② Look at your results. What language areas in this module do you need to study more?

Sound Choice 2

1 **1.17** Grammar - emphatic stress in negation **Listen to the sentences and <u>underline</u> the word which is stressed.**

1 I've got <u>no</u> money.
2 There's very little time left.
3 There aren't any good films on.
4 They give no real evidence.
5 I haven't got any clean clothes.
6 I've got nothing to say.

2 **1.18** Consonants - voiced and unvoiced **Listen and tick (✓) the words you hear.**

1 add	✓	at	☐	6 boat	☐	vote	☐
2 best	☐	vest	☐	7 plays	☐	place	☐
3 back	☐	bag	☐	8 dry	☐	try	☐
4 peace	☐	peas	☐	9 rib	☐	rip	☐
5 post	☐	boast	☐	10 think	☐	thing	☐

3 **1.19** Consonants **Listen and repeat the words.**

1 this   3 vision   5 conclusion   7 music
2 basic   4 thin   6 further   8 health

4 **1.20** Vowels - /ɪ/, /iː/, /æ/, /ʌ/, /e/, /ʊ/ and /ʌ/ **Match the words below with the words that have the same vowel sound (1-7). Then listen to check. One word does not have the same vowel sound as any of the words below.**

bit ~~beat~~ bat but bet book

1 speech   *beat*   5 test   _____
2 cut   _____   6 flame   _____
3 put   _____   7 sing   _____
4 catch   _____

5 **1.21** Vowels - /ɪ/, /iː/, /æ/, /ʌ/, /e/, /ʊ/ and /ʌ/ **Listen and tick (✓) the words you hear.**

1 bit	✓	beat	☐
2 cat	☐	cut	☐
3 mat	☐	met	☐
4 look	☐	luck	☐
5 at	☐	ate	☐
6 hat	☐	hut	☐
7 sit	☐	seat	☐

6 **1.22** Spelling - homophones **Listen to the sentences and choose the correct word.**

1 (weather)/whether   5 buy/by
2 meet/meat   6 piece/peace
3 weak/week   7 hear/here
4 one/won   8 where/wear

7 **1.23** Spelling **Listen and repeat the words. Then write them in the correct column.**

-ence	-ance
difference	_____
_____	_____
_____	_____
_____	

8 **1.24** Expressions - intonation **Listen and repeat the sentences.**

1 There's no doubt that this is true.
2 In my opinion, newspapers are too expensive.
3 I'm sorry but that's just not true.
4 Don't you think so?
5 I wouldn't say that.
6 At first, the woman was scared.
7 The next thing that happens is that the lights go out.
8 In the end, they realise it was a joke.

9 **1.25** Difficult words **Look at the words and <u>underline</u> the silent letters. Then listen and repeat the words.**

1 doubt   5 scientific
2 campaign   6 dialogues
3 whale   7 knee
4 sign   8 government

TOPIC TALK – VOCABULARY

1 Label the pictures.

1

t r a i n e r s

2

t _ _ l _ _ c _ _ p _ t _ _

3

c _ _ m _ _ _ _ _ _

4

j _ _ _ l _ _ _ _

5

s _ _ c _ _

6

h _ _ _ _ h _ _ _
p _ _ d _ _ _ _

7

s _ _ -n _ _

8

w _ _ h _ _ _ p _ w _ _ r

2 Replace the <u>underlined</u> words and phrases with an adjective with a similar meaning.

1 It was <u>boring</u>.　　　d*ull*_____

2 It was <u>unfair to women</u>.　s_____

3 It was <u>funny</u>.　　　h_____/
　　　　　　　　　　　　a_____

4 It was <u>surprising and upset a lot of people</u>.　s_____

5 It was <u>strange</u>.　　　u_____/
　　　　　　　　　　　　w_____

6 It was <u>slightly offensive</u>.　t_____

7 It was <u>not very sensible</u>.　s_____

3 Match the types of advertising (1-7) with the words (a-g).

1 emails which you didn't want or ask for _c_

2 letters which you didn't want or ask for ___

3 companies pay money to have their name associated with certain events ___

4 celebrities say that they use a certain product or are seen in public using it ___

5 adverts on radio or television ___

6 adverts that appear on your computer screen when you visit certain websites ___

7 posters, usually by the side of a road, advertising a product or service ___

a sponsoring　　　**e** endorsements

b billboards　　　**f** junk mail

c spam　　　　　**g** commercials

d pop-ups

4 Complete the dialogue with the words below.

annoy　around　bargain　~~commercials~~　funny
influence　junk mail　reviews　spam　website

Nathan: Oh no. Adverts again. I can't concentrate on a film when there are ¹ _commercials_ in the middle of it.

Ray: I like this one. It's quite ² _____ .

Nathan: Yes, some ads are good but they ³ _____ me when I'm watching a film and a lot of them are rubbish.

Ray: They don't worry me. The adverts I hate are ⁴ _____ ads, you know that pop up when you're online. I can't believe they ever ⁵ _____ anyone to buy something. I just click to close them without thinking.

Nathan: I sometimes read ⁶ _____ because I love getting letters in the post. I read ⁷ _____ emails, too. I still hope that I will find a ⁸ _____ one day but I never do.

Ray: Do you read adverts when you are shopping ⁹ _____ for something important?

Nathan: No, you can't trust adverts. I read ¹⁰ _____ of products online. They're more honest.

13 The Passive

REMEMBER

Complete Exercises A–B before you start this lesson.

A Choose the correct verb form, active or passive, to complete the sentences.

1 The advert *showed/was shown* for the first time last night.
2 I've never *influenced/been influenced* by an advert.
3 *Do you shop/Are you shopped* around?
4 More people should *complain/be complained* about dishonest advertising.
5 Can pop-ups *stop/be stopped*?
6 I like commercials which *tell/are told* a story.
7 Billboards should *ban/be banned* near busy roads.
8 Millions of pounds *spend/are spent* on some advertising campaigns.
9 Soon adverts *will show/will be shown* during the news.
10 Celebrities *pay/are paid* a lot of money to appear in adverts.

B Choose the correct modal.

1 I _c_ buy this coffee if it was cheaper.
   a can   **b** will   **c** would
2 You ___ make people look better in photos by using programmes like Photoshop.
   a will   **b** can   **c** must
3 Our new advertising campaign is going to start next week and I'm sure it ___ be very successful.
   a might   **b** must   **c** will
4 Advertisers ___ follow the government's new rules on honesty.
   a must   **b** would   **c** can
5 They ___ make cosmetics more environmentally friendly if they wanted to.
   a can   **c** might   **c** could
6 They ___ not sell this product in the shops. It depends on how successful their online sales are.
   a could   **b** might   **c** will

1 * Complete the sentences with the verb forms below.

> do / buy   ~~has been bought~~   have bought
> is / bought   will be bought   will buy

1 This product _has been bought_ by millions of people since it went on sale.
2 I'm sure lots of people _____ this product in the future.
3 _____ this product often _____ by men?
4 Lots of people _____ this product since it went on sale.
5 _____ men often _____ this product?
6 I'm sure this product _____ by lots of people in the future.

> can be persuaded   can persuade   has / persuaded
> have / been persuaded   persuaded   was persuaded

7 We _____ people to buy anything.
8 _____ an advert ever _____ you to buy anything?
9 I saw an advert for shampoo on the television last week and I _____ to buy it.
10 People _____ to buy anything.
11 An advert for shampoo that I saw on the television _____ me to buy it.
12 _____ you ever _____ to buy something because of an advert?

2 * Complete the text with the verbs in brackets in the correct passive form.

1 Adverts for toys _are often shown_ (often show) during children's programmes.
2 A new billboard _____ (put up) at the end of our street at the moment.
3 Last week we _____ (ask) to try some chocolate and say what we thought about it in our local supermarket.
4 _____ (you ever / trick) by a dishonest advert?
5 This product _____ (going to / sell) all over the world so we need a good name for it.
6 The government hopes a new law on advertising _____ (will / agree) soon.
7 Pop-ups _____ (can / easily / prevent).
8 Companies _____ (should / stop) from making false promises.
9 I want _____ (tell) the truth by companies, not lies.
10 I hate _____ (send) junk mail which says 'Congratulations, you have won a prize'.

❸ ** Complete the text with the correct passive form of the verbs below.

already / see   choose   copy   download
~~record~~   see   show (x 2)   talk   think

TV programmes can now [1] _be recorded_ without the adverts. Programs can also [2]_____ which will stop pop-ups on your computer. It is becoming harder and harder for companies to guarantee that adverts for their products will [3]_____ . Or is it?
The car company, Volkswagen may disagree. In 2011, they produced an advert for their cars which [4]_____ on American television during the Super Bowl. However, the advert [5]_____ by over a million people on YouTube in the week before the Super Bowl. The company had deliberately allowed it [6]_____ early and, by the time it appeared on television it [7]_____ about all over the country. Why? Because it was cleverly made, fun and more like a short film than an advert.
The slogan which [8]_____ by the company for the advertising campaign was 'The force' which [9]_____ from the *Star Wars* films. The adverts showed characters from the films and was very entertaining. It [10]_____ that about 65 million people have seen the commercial, more than twice as many as the second most popular commercial of the year.

❹ *** Complete the second sentence so that it has a similar meaning to the first.

1 We will put the exam results on the noticeboard.
   The exam results _will be put on the noticeboard._

2 They should tell us the truth.
   We _____

3 You must clean the machinery once a week.
   The machinery _____

4 They were paying celebrities to endorse the product.
   Celebrities _____

5 They aren't going to persuade anybody to buy this product.
   No one _____

6 They are lying to you.
   You _____

7 They can't show adverts for alcohol on the television.
   Adverts for alcohol _____

8 You need to change the batteries every week.
   The batteries _____

Grammar Alive
Giving product information

❺ *** Complete the dialogue using the cues in brackets.

A: Hello, I'm looking for a camera. Would you recommend this one?

B: Not really. [1] _It can't be used at night._ (It / can't use / at night) as it hasn't got a flash.

A: Oh. What about the batteries? Do they last a long time?

B: No. [2]_____
(They / must / change / after an hour)

A: Is it cheap?

B: Not really. [3]_____
(The price / go up / twice / since June)

A: Are the instructions easy to follow?

B: Well, [4]_____
(the instructions / not include / in the box)

A: Where are they?

B: [5]_____
(They / have to / download / from the internet)
Would you like to buy the camera?

A: No, I don't think so, thank you.

❻ *** Complete the questions for the answers.

1 **A:** Have these cosmetics _been tested on animals?_
   B: No, we don't test any of our cosmetics on animals.

2 **A:** Can _____ on children?
   B: Oh yes. You can use this shampoo on babies. It's very gentle.

3 **A:** Where is _____ ?
   B: Lots of shops sell this soap. Supermarkets, chemist's, it's easy to find.

4 **A:** Should these tablets _____ ?
   B: No, not in the morning because they make you tired. Just take one before you go to bed.

5 **A:** Was _____ ?
   B: No, not in England. Not many computers are made here. This one was made in Japan.

14

SKILLS
Reading

1 Read the texts quickly and match the sentences (a-f) with the texts they refer to (1-2).

a It saves you working. _2_

b It looks great. ___

c It helps your family stay healthy. ___

d It is very quick. ___

e It knows where it has been. ___

f It comes with helpful advice. ___

1

Something for the summer

More and more parents are concerned about what their children eat but, when the summer comes and the temperatures rise, there is only one thing that kids want – a tasty ice cream or an ice lolly. One, every now and then, is fine but when kids eat them all the time, it means they are eating a lot of sugar. That's why it is good to make your own ices and that has now become a lot easier with the Zoku Quick Pop Maker. It is easy to use and your lollies don't need to be made the day before you want them. With the Pop Maker, they are ready in minutes. The useful recipe book that comes free with the machine helps you to make a wide variety of flavours using fresh fruit juice, yoghurt and other, less healthy ingredients. In fact, your kids will have as wide a choice as in the shops. Your kids will love their daily lolly and you'll love to see them eating healthy food. Get your Zoku Quick Pop Maker now before the summer comes.

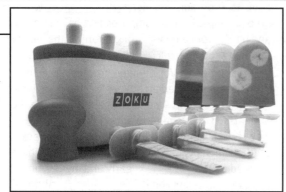

2

Are your floors dirty again?
Are you sick and tired of getting on your knees to clean up?
Don't worry. The Evolution Robotics Mint Floor Cleaner will clean them for you.

Great technology

The cleaner uses the most modern technology to find its way around your rooms. It never misses a centimetre. It will work around furniture and clean right up to the walls. When it has finished, it will return to the place it started and switch itself off so you know exactly when the room is ready.

Stylish and easy to use

The cleaner is small, light and very elegant looking. Measuring 20 cm x 20 cm and 8 cm high it weighs just 3 kg and the noise level when it is working is very low. The battery lasts for about two hours before it needs recharging. The machine doesn't clean very quickly but it does clean very well.

Save money

Unlike vacuum cleaners, there are no expensive bags which need changing every month. The cleaner uses dry and wet cloths which can be washed again and again. Use the dry cloth first to clean hairs and dust and then the wet cloth to make the floor shine.

Don't worry!

The amazing technology means that the cleaner will never fall downstairs or try to clean the carpets. It knows exactly where it can and can't go.

Get your Evolution Robotics Mint Floor Cleaner today and throw away your old buckets once and for all!

2 Read the texts again and choose the correct answers.

1 What does the first text say is wrong with shop bought ice lollies?
  a They are expensive.
  b They are unhealthy.
  c There isn't enough variety.
  d They stop children eating their meals.

2 Which of these is <u>not</u> mentioned as an advantage of the Pop Maker?
  a It is quick.
  b It is simple to use.
  c You can use a variety of different ingredients.
  d It is cheap.

3 The booklet
  a only gives healthy recipe ideas.
  b doesn't cost anything.
  c can be bought on its own.
  d tells you how to make ice creams that are sold in shops.

4 The Evolution Robotics Mint Floor Cleaner
  a cleans better than other machines.
  b doesn't miss any parts of the floor when it cleans.
  c is quicker than other cleaners.
  d uses less energy than other cleaners.

5 One problem with the cleaner is that
  a it needs new batteries very often.
  b it is big and heavy.
  c it makes a lot of noise.
  d the batteries need recharging quite often

6 The main selling point in the second text is that
  a the cleaner will make your life easier.
  b the cleaner will save you money.
  c your house will be cleaner.
  d the cleaner is environmentally friendly.

3 Match sentences 1-4 with texts 1-2.

1 It is easy to read. _2_
2 There is a lot of factual information. ___
3 It includes negative facts which makes it more believable. ___
4 It looks more like a review or a message from a happy customer than an advert. ___

Word Builder Word pairs

4 Complete the sentences with one word in each gap.

1 We use more and ___more___ machines in our day-to-day lives.
2 Sooner or _____ , you're going to have to buy a new laptop.
3 Mobile phones have made face-to-_____ communication less important.
4 I worry about the future now and _____ but not very often.
5 I'm sick and _____ of the pop-up adverts on this website.
6 I've travelled far and _____ but this is the place I'll always come back to.
7 My camera isn't perfect but, by and _____ , I'm happy with it.
8 Unfortunately, we can't pick and _____ the adverts that we see.
9 I'd like someone to put a stop to junk mail once and for _____ .

Sentence Builder need

5 Continue what each person says using the correct form of *need* and the verb in brackets. Don't change the form of the verb in brackets.

1 The kitchen light is still on.
  It needs switching off.
  (it / switching off)
2 I couldn't go for a cycle ride at the weekend.
  _____
  (my bike / checked) first but no one had time to do it.
3 These white walls are starting to look a bit yellow.
  _____
  (they / painted / next year).
4 The printer isn't working.
  _____
  (you / think / ink / changing?)
5 You can't eat these potatoes.
  _____
  (they / cooked / first!)
6 I'm not sure about my hair.
  _____
  (you / think / cutting?)
7 Why are my jeans in the washing machine?
  _____
  (they / not / washing)
8 Your desk is a mess.
  _____
  _____
  (it / tidying / last week and / still / tidying now)

Oral Skills

Listening

1 **1.26** Listen to three people talking. Match the sentences (1-8) with the people they refer to. Write S (Simon), N (Natalie) or T (Terry).

1 He/She is searching for information about mobile phones. _N_

2 He/She is worried that the computer might get a virus. ___

3 He/She offers to help. ___

4 He/She knows how to close the pop-up advert. ___

5 He/She recommends a website. ___

6 He/She opens a website which causes a problem. ___

7 He/She doesn't know what a virus checker is. ___

8 He/She offers to clean the virus. ___

2 **1.27** Listen to the extracts from the dialogue and choose the correct meaning for the words below.

1 fear: *be happy/be worried*

2 invisible: *impossible to see/strange-looking*

3 fake: *not real/not interesting*

4 dodgy: *dishonest/useless*

5 solve (a problem): *cause a problem/find the answer to a problem*

Sentence Builder Preferences

3 Make responses from the cues.

1 **A:** Can I go out?
   B: I / rather / you / stay at home
   I'd rather you stayed at home.

2 **A:** Do you want to play a computer game?
   B: I / prefer / watch / a DVD.
   _____

3 **A:** This is a good film, isn't it?
   B: Yes, but I / rather / there / not be / so many adverts
   _____

4 **A:** Are you glad it's Friday?
   B: Yes, but / I / prefer / it / be / Saturday
   _____

5 **A:** Hey, how was your date last night?
   B: I / rather / not talk / about it
   _____

6 **A:** David will try to fix your old computer.
   B: I / rather / he / buy / me a new one!
   _____

Speaking

1 **1.28** Look at the underlined sentences and decide how many words the sentence could be reduced to (a-c). Then listen to check and write the shortened sentence.

1 **A:** Can I ask you a question?
   B: Of course you can.
      a 2   **b** 3   **c** 1
      Of course.

2 **A:** Have you checked the batteries?
   B: Yes, I have checked the batteries.
      a 3   **b** 4   **c** 2
      _____

3 **A:** Hello. Is there anybody there?
      a 2   **b** 3   **c** 4
      _____

4 **A:** Thanks for your help.
   B: It was no problem for me.
      a 4   **b** 2   **c** 3
      _____

5 **A:** Do you think there is something wrong with my virus checker?
   B: That could be the problem.
      a 2   **b** 3   **c** 1
      _____

2 Reduce the sentences (1-8) by crossing out the number of words in brackets.

A: Hello, ¹Is anybody there? (1)

B: Hello. ²Is there anything I can do for you? (2)

A: It's my computer. It's been really slow recently.

B: ³Since when has it been running slowly? (5)

A: ⁴It has been running slowly since last week. (5). I downloaded some free programmes to clean the computer. Do you think they could be the problem?

B: ⁵They could be the cause of the problem. (6)

A: And yesterday the screen went blue.

B: ⁶Did it go blue? (2)

A: Yes and there was a message about the problem.

B: Do you know what it was?

A: ⁷I am afraid not. (2) Do you think it's completely dead?

B: ⁸I don't think so. (1) I'm sure it'll be all right. I'll have a look at it and you can collect it on Tuesday. Okay?

A: Great. Thanks.

16
GRAMMAR
Nouns

1 * Complete the sentences with the correct form of the word in brackets.

1 Use MouthShine Toothpaste for perfect, white _____teeth_____ (tooth).

2 Why do adverts always show _____ (woman) in the kitchen and never _____ (man)?

3 I don't think _____ (child) should watch TV commercials.

4 I need a lot of _____ (information) about household products for a project I'm doing.

5 How many _____ (person) actually open spam emails?

6 On this game show, two _____ (family) have to answer questions.

7 Carole dyed her _____ (hair) and now she's blonde.

8 There are two really good _____ (series) on television at the moment.

2 ** Decide which sentence in each pair (a–b) could be rewritten by replacing the <u>underlined</u> words with the phrase below.

1 a <u>The class</u> are very well behaved.
   b <u>This class</u> is smaller than it was in September.
   The students in this class _a_

2 a <u>The team</u> get on very well together.
   b <u>This team</u> has got a lot of star players.
   The players on this team ___

3 a <u>My family</u> is very big.
   b <u>My family</u> meet together every Sunday.
   The people in my family ___

4 a <u>The film crew</u> work very hard.
   b <u>The film crew</u> was split in half because the studio needed two crews.
   The members of the film crew ___

5 a <u>The staff</u> is surprisingly small for such a big school.
   b <u>Our staff</u> are happy to help you.
   The members of staff ___

6 a <u>The company</u> are trying hard to provide a good service.
   b <u>The company</u> is having financial problems.
   The people in the company ___

3 ** Choose the correct word.

1 Be quiet, the news (is)/are on.

2 My trousers *is/are* too short.

3 Be careful. The stairs *is/are* very dangerous.

4 Where did you buy *this/these* clothes?

5 Can you give me *that/those* scissors, please?

6 Your hair *look/looks* beautiful.

7 The police always *come/comes* immediately if you phone them.

8 *Is this/Are these* enough money for a ticket?

4 *** Complete the sentences with one word from the pairs below.

news / articles   brains / mind   hair / hairs
clothes / dress   ~~staff / teacher~~   advice / tips
knife / scissors   tooth / teeth   foot / feet
histories / story

1 The _____staff_____ at this school are all very helpful.

2 I cut myself with this _____ .

3 My left _____ hurt after I ran 10 km.

4 This is an interesting _____ about life in the nineteenth century.

5 These _____ don't fit me. I'll have to go on a diet.

6 He's got a very good _____ and can work out difficult scientific problems.

7 You should get your _____ checked by the dentist every six months.

8 There are a lot of interesting _____ in this newspaper.

9 Thanks for the _____ – it was very useful and helped me sort out my problem.

10 Could you clean these _____ out of the bath, please. They're definitely yours!

Writing Workshop 4

1 Look at the letter of complaint and choose the best summary for each paragraph (A-D).

A *The reason for writing./Thanking the company for their product.*

B *Details about the product./Problems with the product.*

C *Suggestions on how to improve customer service./Problems with contacting the company.*

D *What the writer wants from the company./Legal advice for the company.*

Dear Sir/Madam,

A I am writing to complain about a pair of walking boots that I bought from your website on April 10th this year. They are the Eeze-hike boots, size 44. I enclose the receipt and internet advertisement.

B In your advertisement, you claim that the boots are waterproof. However, when I went walking in the rain, my socks quickly became wet and the walk was very uncomfortable. The boots are also not 100% leather as you stated. They are a mixture of leather and plastic. Finally, you stated that the boots were available in black, brown or red. I chose black but received a pair of brown boots.

C When I phoned the contact number on your website, I was asked to wait. I waited for ten minutes and, no sooner had my call been answered by someone than I was asked to wait again. I hung up as the call cost 50p a minute and decided to write instead.

D Not only would I like a refund of my money but I would also like an apology for my inconvenience and discomfort when wearing your boots. Unless I hear from you in the next few weeks, I will have to take further action. I have been reading about consumer rights on the internet and I believe I could actually request more than a simple refund if I wished to.

I look forward to hearing from you.

Yours faithfully,

Michael Jacobs

Sentence Builder Emphasis (2)

2 Read the text again and complete the two sentences.

1 Not only _____ refund of my money _____ an apology for my inconvenience.

2 No sooner _____ by someone _____ to wait again.

3 Choose the correct words to complete the sentences.

1 Not only _b_ too big, but they are broken.

  a they are   **b** are they

2 Not only ___ written to you but I have also written to my lawyer.

  a have I   **b** I have

3 Not only ___ to send the telephone, but you also promised to send a free MP3 player.

  a you promised   **b** did you promise

4 No sooner ___ than the adverts came on.

  a the film started   **b** had the film started

5 No sooner ___ than we realised we had forgotten our lunch.

  a had we left   **b** did we leave

4 You bought a DVD from the internet. There are several things wrong with it. Read the instructions below and write a letter of complaint to the company.

- It didn't have a second disc of extras as it said in the advert.
- It was scratched.
- It took two weeks to arrive even though you paid for express delivery (guaranteed to arrive the next day).

Write between 150 and 180 words.

Check Your Progress 4

1 Advertising **Complete the answers to the questions with one letter in each gap.**

1 **A:** What kind of advert was it?
   B: It was a b _ _ _ b _ _ r _ next to the main road.

2 **A:** What product was it advertising?
   B: It was advertising health and b _ _ u _ _ products.

3 **A:** What did you think of it?
   B: It was quite t _ _ t _ l _ _ _ and sexist.

4 **A:** What kind of advertising really annoys you?
   B: I hate d _ _ _ c _ mail, you know junk mail.

5 **A:** What's the best way to advertise?
   B: I like celebrity e _ _ _ r _ _ m _ _ t _ .

6 **A:** Any other ideas?
   B: Well, s _ _ n _ _ r _ _ _ events like the World Cup or the Olympics.

/6

2 The Passive **Complete the dialogue with the correct form of the verbs in brackets.**

A: How much should we charge for this newspaper?
B: It could ¹_____ (give) away free.
A: How would we make any money?
B: We will ²_____ (pay) by advertisers.
A: I see. It might work. Okay, let's look at this report. It ³_____ (write) last week. It looks at different newspapers.
B: Sorry to interrupt you but a lot of mistakes ⁴_____ (make) by the writers. A new report ⁵_____ (prepare) at the moment.
A: What? Why ⁶_____ (I not tell) about this? I've been reading this report all morning ready for this meeting.

/6

3 Word pairs **Complete the sentences with one word in each gap.**

1 N_____ and then, I find an article in this magazine that really interests me.
2 I'm s_____ and tired of celebrity gossip.
3 We should decide who is the best writer o_____ and for all.
4 S_____ or later, newspapers are going to disappear.
5 We searched f_____ and wide for a reliable team of workers and now they've left us.
6 You can't p_____ and choose who is going to be in your class at school.

/6

4 Nouns **Complete the sentences with the correct word or words from the pairs below.**

is/are   has been/have been   need/needs
stop/stops   this/these   was/were

1 This information _____ out of date.
2 The news _____ very bad recently.
3 The trousers I bought _____ a bargain.
4 My hair _____ cutting.
5 The police often _____ my brother when he's cycling.
6 Where did you get _____ clothes?

/6

5 Emphasis (2) **Complete the second sentence so that it has the same meaning as the first.**

1 We got home and my brother immediately switched on his computer.
   No sooner _____

2 I read the newspaper and I watch the TV news.
   Not only _____

3 I went to the gym and I jogged home.
   Not only _____

4 I opened the newspaper and saw my dad's photo.
   No sooner _____

5 My sister saw the advert for shampoo and rushed out to buy some.
   No sooner _____

6 These cosmetics are environmentally friendly and good for your skin.
   Not only _____

/6

TOTAL SCORE   /30

Module Diary

1 Look at the objectives on page 35 in the Students' Book. Choose three and evaluate your learning.

1 Now I can _____
   well / quite well / with problems.

2 Now I can _____
   well / quite well / with problems.

3 Now I can _____
   well / quite well / with problems.

2 Look at your results. What language areas in this module do you need to study more?

Exam Choice 2

Reading

1 Read the text quickly and match the names (1-5) with the facts (a-e).

1 Volkswagen ___
2 BMW Z3 ___
3 Apple products ___
4 A Wilson volleyball ___
5 Jim Carrey ___

a appeared in a film which laughed at product placement.
b spent $200 million on product placement in 2002.
c was/were found by Tom Hanks in a film.
d appeared in the James Bond film *GoldenEye*.
e often appear(s) in cartoons.

WHAT IS
PRODUCT PLACEMENT?

It is a form of advertising in films or television programmes. [1]___ A company pays for the director or writer to use their product. In many films characters eat, drink, drive cars and do other everyday activities. It is very good for the film-makers if they can be paid to use certain products that they would need anyway. [2]___ . Even though people watching a film aren't concentrating on the products, they do notice them. That's why people are prepared to pay a lot of money for this kind of advertising. It is thought that, in 2010, almost $2 billion was spent on placing products in films. Volkswagen alone spent about $200 million on product placement in 2002. [3]___ The BMW Z3 was used in the film *GoldenEye*. After the film came out, sales of the car increased greatly. In fact, cars are the most popular product to be placed in films. They are also often placed in computer games, especially racing games.

Other products often placed include computers, food, drinks and restaurants. Interestingly, Apple products often appear in newspaper cartoon stories.
[4]___ Perhaps Apple are popular because, rather than paying cash for product placement, they offer their products. Cartoonists obviously like creating their work on Apple computers.

Product placement is usually quite difficult to notice. The Bond film-makers might have used a BMW Z3 anyway. The car suits the character. Characters in films would naturally eat and drink popular brands. Does it matter if one character opens a fridge door and there are several cans of a popular soft drink? Does it matter if the camera spends a few seconds longer than is necessary filming the cans?

[5]___ In the film, Cast Away, Tom Hanks, alone on an island, finds a Wilson volleyball. He names it Wilson. [6]___ 'Wilson, Wilson.' Even worse is when films, books or television shows are written specially to include the products being advertised. There is a danger that they may then become a 90-minute, or a 300-page advert, rather than a film or a book.

One film that made fun of product placement was the Jim Carrey comedy *The Truman Show*. Unknown to Truman, his whole life was turned into a reality TV show. He couldn't see the cameras and didn't realise he was being filmed. [7]___ One thing did make him suspicious, though. His wife and best friend had a strange habit of holding up products and saying their names very loudly for no reason at all.

The Truman Show was a comedy and people laughed at how ridiculous it looked. One day, if advertisers get their way, it may not look very different to any other film.

2 **Read the text again. Match the sentences (a-h) with the gaps (1-7). There is one extra sentence.**

- **a** It is also good for the advertisers.
- **b** This is why it is so effective.
- **c** Sometimes, though, product placement can become too obvious.
- **d** It can even be found in books.
- **e** Everyone else knew except him.
- **f** In one scene he calls its name several times.
- **g** James Bond films are very popular with car makers.
- **h** Apart from these, product placement in this kind of media is very rare.

Listening

3 **[1.29] Listen to three people discussing the news. Match the people with the sentences (1-8). Write A (Amy), J (John) or M (Matt).**

1 He/She has got a newspaper. ___
2 He/She buys a newspaper for his/her father. ___
3 He/She only reads online newspapers. ___
4 He/She doesn't believe what he/she reads in the newspaper. ___
5 He/She believes there are aliens in Scotland. ___
6 He/She sometimes watches the news on television with his/her parents. ___
7 He/She doesn't like 24-hour news programmes. ___
8 He/She thinks that television news is not real. ___

4 **[1.29] Listen again. Are the sentences true (T) or false (F)?**

1 John read three articles in the newspaper. ___
2 John reads the newspaper at home. ___
3 Matt doesn't think you can find the truth anywhere on the internet. ___
4 John agrees with Matt about the government and aliens. ___
5 Amy likes watching the news at ten o'clock. ___
6 John doesn't think people should watch 24-hour news channels for a long time. ___
7 Matt prefers watching the news on television to reading newspapers. ___
8 Amy doesn't think it is a good idea for Matt to keep looking at the websites he likes. ___

Speaking

5 **Complete the description of an advert with the words below. There are four extra words.**

end   eventually   finally   first   firstly   happens
just   next   ridiculous   scene   then

The ¹_____ starts off with a lion hunting for food. At ²_____ it looks like a nature documentary. The lion is chasing a zebra. It's ³_____ hilarious because we then see the lion suddenly stop and enter a supermarket to buy some meat. A man speaking says that lions only eat the freshest meat and they know where to get it. The ⁴_____ thing that ⁵_____ is that the lion walks out of the supermarket where the zebra is waiting for it. It's ⁶_____ because the zebra tries to get the lion to chase it again and looks really sad when the lion is uninterested. In the ⁷_____ , the zebra goes into the supermarket and asks if they sell fresh grass.

6 **Look at the conversation between a customer in a mobile phone shop and a salesperson. Complete the conversation with the words below.**

have   didn't   anything   problem
since   course   anybody   afraid

Customer: Hello. ¹_____ there?
Salesperson: Good morning. ²_____ I can do for you?
Customer: Yes, it's this phone. It's stopped working.
Salesperson: ³_____ when?
Customer: About three days ago. I left it in the garden overnight.
Salesperson: You ⁴_____ !
Customer: Yes, and it rained. Do you think you can fix it?
Salesperson: ⁵_____ not but you have an account with us so I can give you a replacement. Have you got a memory card in this one?
Customer: Yes, I ⁶_____ . Could you put it into a new phone for me? I haven't got my glasses and it's very small.
Salesperson: Of ⁷_____ , no ⁸_____ .

Exam Choice 2

Use of English

7 Complete the second sentence so that it has the same meaning as the first. Use 2-6 words including the word in capitals.

1 I was extremely upset when Ellen left me but it could have been worse.
(END)
I was extremely upset when Ellen left me but
_____
the world.

2 My dad never left the house before he had finished reading the Sunday paper.
(USE)
My dad _____
the house before he had finished reading the Sunday paper.

3 Very few adverts are worth watching.
(ANY)
_____
are worth watching.

4 Nothing you say will convince me.
(ANYTHING)
There _____
that will convince me.

5 There were such a lot of adverts that I had time to make a cup of tea.
(SO)
There _____
adverts that I had time to make a cup of tea.

6 I think they wrote this article in about two minutes.
(WAS)
I think this article _____
_____ in about two minutes.

7 I'd prefer you not to use my computer while I'm out.
(RATHER)
I'd _____
my computer while I'm out.

8 It's becoming more normal for me to stay late at school to help with the school newsletter.
(USED)
I'm _____
late at school to help with the school newsletter.

Writing

8 Complete the sentences with one word in each gap.

1 With their _____ of adverts featuring talking meerkats, comparethemarket.com has become famous.

2 There have been so _____ 'meerkat' adverts that it is difficult to say which my favourite is.

3 It is amazing that the advertisers have come up with _____ a lot of ideas.

4 Not _____ are the adverts funny but they are also very clever.

5 No _____ do the adverts appear on television than they go onto YouTube where millions of people watch them.

6 _____ , not everyone likes the talking animals.

7 Worst of _____ , they laugh at people who can't say 'market' properly.

8 To _____ up, they are very funny and popular but perhaps not as good as some people say they are.

9 Read the instructions below and write a review of an advert or series of adverts which are popular in your country. Use the ideas in Exercise 8 if you want to.

- Give basic information about the adverts.
- Say what is good about the adverts.
- Say what is bad about the adverts.
- Write a conclusion showing your opinion about the adverts.

Write between 120 and 180 words.

TOPIC TALK – VOCABULARY

1 **Choose the correct words.**

1 I've broken *a*/my jaw.
2 I've *pulled*/*cut* a muscle.
3 I've *sprained*/*grazed* myself.
4 I've *pulled*/*broken* a rib.
5 I've *strained*/*sprained* a tendon.
6 I've *sprained*/*pulled* my wrist.
7 I've *broken*/*torn* a toe.
8 I've broken *my*/*a* collarbone.

2 **Match the problems (1-8) with the doctor's opinions (a-h).**

1 I find it difficult to breathe. _e_
2 I'm covered in red spots. ___
3 My head hurts so much that I can't see properly. ___
4 I've been sick since I ate some undercooked chicken. ___
5 I feel hot and cold and I've got a high temperature. ___
6 I sneeze all the time in the summer. ___
7 I find it difficult to go to the toilet. ___
8 Since I came back from Africa I've had fevers and headaches. It feels like the flu but worse. ___

a I think you've got salmonella.
b It might be malaria.
c It sounds like flu.
d You suffer from hay fever.
e We'll test you for asthma.
f It's probably a migraine.
g I'm afraid it's chickenpox.
h You've got constipation.

3 **Match the problems (a-h) with the sentences (1-8).**

1 Keith is worried. _e_
2 Emily is very sad. ___
3 Lucy gets angry very easily. ___
4 Dad gets very tense. ___
5 My uncle really needs to sleep. ___
6 Mum's just a bit ill. It's nothing serious. ___
7 Chris doesn't feel like eating anything. ___
8 My brother finds it difficult to do anything in the mornings. ___

He/She:

a is very irritable.
b is feeling under the weather.
c is often stressed out.
d has no appetite.
e is anxious.
f is overtired.
g has no energy.
h is depressed.

4 **Complete the text with the words below.**

attacks bone colds depressed diet
disease edge exercise sleep ~~sprained~~

I've always been lucky with my health. I have
[1] _sprained_ my ankle but I have never broken
a [2]_____ . In the winter, I sometimes get
[3]_____ but I've never had flu. I try and stay
happy and relaxed all the time. I have never felt
[4]_____ but I do occasionally feel a little bit
on [5]_____ , especially just before exams.
To keep healthy, I do regular [6]_____ .
I go running and swimming. I have quite a good
[7]_____ , although sometimes I have fast food
with my friends. My main problem is that I don't get
enough [8]_____ . I go to bed late because
I love surfing the internet.
In my opinion, the most dangerous [9]_____ in
my country is cancer although more and more people
are having heart [10]_____ and getting liver
disease because of their unhealthy lifestyles.

17 SKILLS
Reading

1 Read the text and match the numbers with what they refer to (a–f).

sixteen _b_   twelve thousand ___
fourteen ___   eight ___
nine ___   three ___

a The number of times he was tested for performance-enhancing drugs at one Olympic tournament.

b The total number of medals he won at his first two Olympic Games.

c The number of meals he eats a day.

d The number of eggs he eats for breakfast.

e The number of gold medals he won in his first two Olympic games.

f The number of calories he eats every day while training.

MICHAEL PHELPS

Michael Phelps is a world-class swimmer. He won eight medals at his first Olympics and eight more four years later. Even more remarkably, all eight that he won in that second tournament were gold. With the six gold medals he had already won, that means he won fourteen gold medals in his first two Olympic games. He was so much better than anyone else that some people believed he must be taking performance-enhancing drugs. However, Michael was tested nine times during his second Olympic tournament and passed every test. In fact, the reason for his amazing success may be his diet.

While training, Michael eats an astonishing 12,000 calories every day. Anyone not doing as much exercise as him would soon suffer from serious health problems if they tried to eat the same amount. However, for Michael it seems that the more he eats, the faster and fitter he becomes.

So, what exactly does he eat? Breakfast includes eight eggs, fried onions, mayonnaise and three chocolate pancakes. Lunch consists of a 500g packet of pasta, ham and cheese sandwiches and more mayonnaise as well as energy drinks. His third, and final meal of the day includes another packet of pasta, a pizza and more energy drinks. All these calories are burned off as, between meals, he spends his time training as hard as possible, pushing himself to the limit.

Is this a good diet for a top-level athlete? Not all experts are convinced but some believe that it is. The sugar and energy drinks mean that Michael gets an immediate burst of energy after eating. When this fades, the body starts getting energy from the carbohydrates, allowing him to continue for longer.

However, others question the diet's effects on his long-term health. They also claim that he could produce the same effects by eating a healthier diet. One dietician recommended eating fewer eggs and more fruit and vegetables. Another stated that three large meals a day are not as beneficial as smaller meals with snacks in between. Carbohydrates are the most important 'fuel' for an athlete's body. The more carbohydrates the body has, the longer the energy levels last. Once the carbohydrates have been used up, the body starts burning fat for energy, great for people trying to lose weight but a less efficient way for the body to get energy for exercise.

Not everyone could eat like Michael Phelps, even if they did exactly the same amount of exercise as he does. He just burns calories more quickly. In fact, experts think that he would burn more calories sitting behind a desk for an hour than most people would burn by doing exercise for the same amount of time.

2 **Read the text again. Are the sentences true (T) or false (F)?**

1 Michael won more medals in his first Olympic games than he did in his second. _F_
2 Michael was found to have taken performance-enhancing drugs. ___
3 The amount of food Michael eats doesn't make him less fit. ___
4 He has pasta twice a day. ___
5 Not all experts agree that Michael has the right diet for an athlete. ___
6 One dietician recommended cutting out snacks between meals. ___
7 If you don't eat carbohydrates, there is nowhere for the body to get energy from. ___
8 Michael can eat more than other people because his body uses more calories than they do. ___

3 **Look at these words from the text and decide whether they are nouns (N), verbs (V) or adjectives (A).**

1 suffer (from) _V_
2 burst (of) ___
3 fades ___
4 question ___
5 beneficial ___
6 efficient ___

4 **Replace the <u>underlined</u> words and phrases with the correct form of the words from Exercise 3.**

1 The students' sudden <u>increase in</u> energy, disappeared as the holidays got closer.
   _____ _burst of_ _____
2 My parents <u>asked</u> me about the reason why I was late home.
   _____
3 I <u>experienced the problem of</u> hay fever when I was younger.
   _____
4 Doing exercise will be <u>good</u> for your heart.
   _____
5 I think an <u>excellent</u> way to burn calories is to walk quickly for an hour.
   _____
6 Our chances <u>gradually disappeared</u> during the second half of the match.
   _____

Word Builder Compounds

5 **Choose the correct answer.**

1 He broke the world _a_ for 100 metres.
   a record   **b** class   **c** famous
2 The speed ___ here is 40 kph.
   a rate   **b** record   **c** limit
3 His heart ___ increased a lot when he did some exercise.
   a rate   **b** attack   **c** limit
4 Haemoglobin in our red blood ___ provides oxygen to our muscles.
   a acid   **b** cells   **c** organs
5 The gym facilities here are first-___ .
   a time   **b** tech   **c** rate
6 Don't take performance-___ drugs.
   a winning   **b** reaching   **c** enhancing
7 Your bad diet and stressful lifestyle could have bad long-___ consequences.
   a term   **b** time   **c** level
8 Sports stars nowadays have great hi-___ equipment to help them get fit.
   a level   **b** tech   **c** rate

Sentence Builder Comparatives

6 **Complete the sentences with the correct forms of the pairs of words below.**

early / good   heavy / difficult   ~~long / bad~~
long / far   more / fit   popular / expensive

1 The _____ _longer_ _____ you take these drugs for, the _____ _worse_ _____ it will be for you in the long term.
2 The _____ your bag is, the _____ it is to carry.
3 The _____ a sport is, the _____ the tickets to see it are.
4 The _____ the race went on, the _____ I was behind the other runners.
5 The _____ exercise you do, the _____ you become.
6 The _____ I go to bed, the _____ I feel the next day.

18 GRAMMAR
Future

REMEMBER

Complete Exercises A–B before you start this lesson.

A Complete the gaps with the verbs in brackets using *will* or *going to*.

A: Have you thought about what to do in the summer?

B: Yes, [1] _*I'm going to get*_ (get) a job in July and then I hope I [2]_____ (have) enough money to go on holiday in August.

A: Where do you want to go?

B: Oh, I don't know yet. I [3]_____ (think) about that later. What about you? [4]_____ (you / work) in the same place as last year?

A: No, I [5]_____ (not work) at all. My parents have given me some money so I [6]_____ (travel) around Europe.

B: Wow. Don't forget about me.

A: I [7]_____ (not). Don't worry. I [8]_____ (send) you a postcard.

B Complete the sentences with the verbs below.

> are leaving   is going to leave
> ~~leaves~~   'll leave

1 Come on. The bus _____*leaves*_____ in five minutes.

2 My brother _____ school when he's sixteen.

3 This is boring. I think I _____ in a minute.

4 Come and say goodbye. Your uncle and aunt _____ now.

> is going to start   is starting
> 'll start   starts

5 My mum _____ a new job tomorrow.

6 My brother _____ working harder from next week. That's what he says, anyway.

7 The film we want to see _____ at eight o'clock.

8 Who wants to go first? No one? Okay, I _____ .

1 * Complete the sentences with the words in capitals.

~~BE~~ / DOES / GOING TO / IS / MAY / WILL

1 I'll _____*be*_____ going to the supermarket later. Do you want anything?

2 Don't worry. I'm sure you _____ do well in your exams.

3 What time _____ the train to London leave?

4 I'm _____ get a summer job this year.

5 I _____ be late. If I am, don't wait for me.

6 Mark isn't coming to the cinema. He _____ meeting his cousin at the station this evening.

2 ** Complete the sentences (a–f) with the correct future form of the verbs in brackets. You can only use each of the future forms (1–6) once.

1 ~~will be + -ing~~

2 *will* + infinitive

3 *going to*

4 *may* + infinitive

5 Present Continuous for future arrangements

6 Present Simple for certain futures

a I can't meet you this evening because I_*'ll be working*_ (work) until nine o'clock.

b I _____ (not have) time to phone you this evening. I'll try but I can't promise.

c The film _____ (start) at seven o'clock so let's meet at half past six.

d Dan and I _____ (play) tennis together tomorrow.

e I think _____ (go) to the match. It should be very exciting.

f Paul _____ (not win) this race. He's getting tired already.

3 ** Choose the correct answers.

1 By Saturday, I'll _*c*_ all of the series on DVD.
   a watch **b** be watching **c** have watched

2 I don't think we ___ the tennis tournament.
   a 'll win **b** 'll have won **c** 'll be winning

3 I can't meet you this evening. I'll ___ until bedtime.
   a work **b** have worked **c** be working

4 At eight o'clock we'll ___ to Scotland. We're leaving at 5 p.m. and should arrive at about ten o'clock.
   a drive **b** be driving **c** have driven

5 I think you ___ this CD.
   a 'll like **b** 'll have liked **c** 'll be liking

6 While you're on holiday, I'll ___ in a shop.
   a work **b** have worked **c** be working

7 By the time we get back to school in September, ___ £400!
   a I'll save **b** I'll have saved **c** I'll be saving

4 *** **Use the cues to make two sentences in the future about each picture.**

1

a By / 8 / train / arrive
By 8 o'clock, the train will have arrived.
By 8 o'clock, the train will have arrived.

b At / 8 / passengers / leave station
At 8 o'clock the passengers will be leaving
the station.

2

a By the time I / be / 30, / I / live / France

b By the time I / be / 30, / I / move / France

3

a By / 11, / Dad / fall asleep

b At / 11, / Dad / sleep

4

a Mum / not arrive at work / by 8.30

b Mum / drive / to work / at 8.30

5 *** **Make full sentences from the cues using the Present Perfect + Future Perfect or Future Simple.**

1 When they / finish / playing / we ask / them for their autographs
When they've finished playing, we'll ask them for
their autographs.

2 When / I / eat / this, I / need to do lots of exercise to burn off the calories

3 When the school year / finish / we / do / about 300 hours of homework

4 When I / save / enough money / I / start / my own business

5 By the time you / send / those invitations, / the party / finish

6 When / you / tidy / your room / I / give / you your pocket money

Grammar Alive Planning

6 *** **Make dialogues from the cues.**

A: ¹ _Are you going to watch_
(you / going / watch) this channel all evening?

B: No. ²_____
(I / going / switch off soon). Why?

A: There's a good film on.
³_____
(It / start / in fifteen minutes).
⁴_____
(Carole / come / round) to watch it with me.

B: Okay, when she arrives,
⁵_____
(I / go upstairs) and play computer games.

A: ⁶_____
(I / going / run) in a marathon next year.

B: Really? ⁷_____
(You / have to) do a lot of training.

A: I know. I'm going to run 5 km every day.

B: Wow! By the time you do the marathon,
⁸_____
(you / run / about 1500 km).

A: That's right. Hey, you could do the marathon, too.

B: Oh, I'm sorry. ⁹_____
(I / do / something else) that day.

A: But you don't even know which day it is.

B: I know but, whatever day it is, I know
¹⁰_____
(I / not run / in a marathon).

19 SKILLS
Oral Skills

Listening

1 🔊 **1.30 Listen to someone talking about life expectancy in Japan and complete the sentences.**

1 Life expectancy in Japan is ___83 years___ .

2 Life expectancy started to go up in the _____ .

3 The Japanese knew it was important to reduce the amount of _____ .

4 The Japanese visit a doctor about _____ times a year compared to _____ times a year in the UK.

5 The Japanese could live even longer if more people stopped _____ .

6 35 people out of every 100,000 on Okinawa live to be over _____ .

7 Compared to other Japanese people, Okinawans eat more vegetables and _____ .

8 People who live on Okinawa often spend their free time in their _____ .

2 🔊 **1.30 Listen again and choose the correct answers.**

1 Life expectancy first started rising in Japan because of:
   a better medical treatment
   b health insurance
   c changes to their diet

2 In Japan there is little difference in life expectancy between:
   a men and women
   b rich and poor
   c old and young

3 There is a growing problem in Japan of:
   a being overweight
   b being stressed
   c people smoking

4 Okinawa is:
   a a Japanese city
   b an island that is part of Japan
   c an independent island near Japan

5 Okinawans are healthy because of:
   a their diet and lifestyle
   b their diet only
   c their lifestyle and the clean air

6 Young people on Okinawa are:
   a leaving for western countries
   b changing their lifestyle
   c suffering from diseases

Speaking

1 **Choose the correct words.**

1 I *think*/*feel*/*mean* so because …
2 *Therefore*/*Because*/*Reason* of that, we need to …
3 That's *reason*/*means*/*why* I think we should …
4 The *fact*/*opinion*/*reason* for that is that …
5 *Therefore*/*Because of*/*The fact*, I think we should …
6 The *fact*/*That means*/*That's why* is that …

2 🔊 **1.31 Complete the sentences with one word in each gap. Then listen to check your answers.**

A: Some people, even in rich countries, are unhealthy. The main [1]*reason* for that is because of their lifestyles and diet. People should care more about their health.

B: It's not that easy. Some ingredients, such as salt, are addictive. [2]_____ fact _____ that people can't stop eating fast food even if they want to. That's [3]_____ I _____ that governments should do something about food companies.

A: As far as I'm concerned, it's not the government's problem. The [4]_____ is _____ we are responsible for our own health.

B: So, what about cigarettes? Don't you think they should be banned?

A: No, it's …

B: But they are really bad for people.

A: Could you let me finish, please? I know they are very unhealthy. [5]_____ , I agree that they should be banned in public places. However, in people's private homes, they can do what they like.

B: The problem is that healthcare costs a fortune. [6]_____ of _____ , I think we [7]_____ to ban cigarettes and put the price of fast food and alcohol up.

A: So why not put the price of cigarettes up, too? That's what I think should happen. I [8]_____ so _____ the government could then use that money for hospitals. Don't you agree?

GRAMMAR
Time reference in the past

❶ * Choose the correct words.

1 In the early nineteenth century, people travelled by horse. The car *wasn't to*/*isn't to* appear for almost a century.

2 I *am going to*/*was going to* eat something healthy but I didn't have time to cook.

3 They lived in a small village where everyone *cooks*/*cooked* healthy meals with food they *grow*/*grew* themselves.

4 When I was sixteen, I thought I *would be*/*will be* an actor one day.

5 I went to Tuscany where I *learned*/*learn* to cook traditional Italian meals.

6 It was obvious that they *will leave*/*would leave* their home to find work.

7 It was a long, dry summer. They didn't know it then but the rain *isn't to*/*wasn't to* appear for another two years.

8 We *were going to*/*are going to* eat less fast food last year but a new restaurant opened near our house and we went there a lot.

❷ * Match the beginnings (1-6) with the correct endings (a-f).

1 I was going _d_
2 I knew he didn't ___
3 I knew you had ___
4 I knew you would ___
5 I knew you were ___
6 It was to ___

a forgotten our meeting.
b be many years before they found out the truth.
c understand what he had to do.
d to send you an email but I forgot.
e going to be angry.
f be the first to arrive.

❸ ** Complete the dialogue with one word in each gap.

A: In the 1960s, my grandparents still ate fast food with a knife and fork! They didn't realise that American style fast food ¹_____was_____ to change eating habits forever. Within twenty years, young people ²_____ be eating burgers with their fingers.

B: Wait a minute. Eating with your fingers isn't new. When our grandparents were young, people ³_____ food with their fingers. They ate fish and chips while they were walking down the road. It wasn't how they ate that changed but what they ate. What they didn't realise then was that a lot of fish and chip shops ⁴_____ close down and become burger bars or fried chicken places in the future.

A: That's true and they're even more surprised by all the food from other countries that people eat now.

B: Definitely. Our grandparents grew up in a country where spaghetti ⁵_____ a strange foreign food and pizzas ⁶_____ unknown. Foreign travel wasn't ⁷_____ become popular until they were in their thirties or forties.

A: Foreign travel hasn't changed their diets much. My grandfather eats the same food wherever he goes - English breakfasts, egg and chips and things like that. He was ⁸_____ to go abroad last summer but when he found out that there were no English restaurants in the resort he decided to stay in England!

❹ *** Complete the sentences with one word in each gap. Use the verbs below in the correct form.

be (x 3) not be come fail ~~forget~~
not go rain wait ~~wear~~

1 **A:** I'm sorry. I didn't buy you a present.
  B: I knew you _would_ _forget_ my birthday.

2 **A:** Hi, I'm ready to go out.
  B: I knew you _were_ _going_ _to_ _wear_ that shirt. You always do.

3 **A:** Mark's in hospital.
  B: Really? I knew he _____ ill but I didn't know it _____ that bad.

4 **A:** Sorry to hear about your exam results.
  B: It wasn't a surprise. I knew I
  _____ _____ _____ _____ .

5 **A:** I've just seen Paul outside the library. He's waiting for you. He's been there for two hours.
  B: Really? I knew he _____ _____ for me but I didn't know I _____ that late.

6 **A:** I'm really tired.
  B: I knew you _____ _____ to bed early enough last night.

7 **A:** Hi Sally, this weather's awful. Why didn't you bring your umbrella?
  B: Hi Tina. I didn't know it _____ _____ _____ _____ today.

8 **A:** Hi, Stella. This is a great party, isn't it?
  B: Hi, Tina. Yes, it is. I didn't think you
  _____ _____ _____ _____ .
  A: I _____ but I changed my mind at the last minute.

Writing Workshop 5

1 Look at the summary of what each paragraph does (1-4) and put the paragraphs of the opinion essay (A-D) in the correct order.

1 introduces the topic _C_
2 gives arguments against labelling ___
3 gives arguments for labelling ___
4 concludes the essay with the writer's point of view ___

All packaged food should be labelled with information about what it contains and how healthy or unhealthy it is.

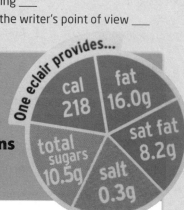

One eclair provides...

cal 218 | fat 16.0g | sat fat 8.2g | salt 0.3g | total sugars 10.5g

A

Some food companies are against the idea. ¹W_hile_____ they say they recognise the importance of a healthy diet, they do not believe that labelling will help. They think the information would be too complicated and might even cause people to have a worse diet ²b_____ they may choose a packaged meal that looks healthy instead of fresh food which has no labelling.

B

To sum up, ³a_____ not everyone will read or understand the information on labels, I think it would be useful ⁴s_____ those of us who do care about our health could then make correct decisions about what we eat.

C

One of the biggest health-related problems in many western countries is caused by our diets. We are overweight ⁵a_____ we eat too much fat. We also suffer from high blood pressure ⁶d_____ to eating too much salt. One idea is to label all packaged foods so that people can see exactly what they are eating.

D

However, many people disagree. ⁷F_____ of all, people are more intelligent than food companies say. ⁸S_____, the information doesn't have to be complicated. An easy traffic lights system has been suggested. Green would mean healthy ⁹w_____ red would mean unhealthy. This system has been criticised because it is too simple. ¹⁰N_____, most people believe it would help.

2 Complete the text with one word in each gap. You can see the first letter of each word.

3 Choose the word or words which can be used in the gap. Sometimes only one word is possible, sometimes two words can be used.

1 Local councils need to do something _a, b_ our children need protecting.
   a because
   b as
   c while

2 Students can go to these restaurants every day _____ many of them are located close to schools.
   a due to
   b because
   c since

3 _____ I understand that we live in a free society, sometimes laws are necessary.
   a Nevertheless
   b Although
   c While

4 Children are more likely to eat unhealthy food. _____, they are more likely to leave the safety of the school grounds.
   a Whereas
   b Although
   c In addition

5 Local restaurant owners give several reasons why they are against the law. _____, they say that longer distances make it more likely that children will have to cross busy roads.
   a In addition
   b First of all
   c While

6 We all know that fast food is unhealthy. _____, I don't think this law would make much difference to children's eating habits.
   a although
   b Nevertheless
   c Whereas

4 Look at the essay topic and read the instructions below. Write an opinion essay. You can also use the sentences from Exercise 3 to help you.

Some towns have banned fast food restaurants from opening closer than 400 metres to schools and parks. Is this a good idea?

- Introduce the topic.
- Give reasons why some people may be against it.
- Give reasons why some people are for it.
- Sum up the essay with your opinions.

Write between 120 and 180 words.

Check Your Progress 5

1 Well-being Complete the words.

Health problems

1 lung c_____
2 heart a_____
3 hay f_____
4 have a high t_____
5 feel under the w_____
6 have no a_____

/6

2 Compounds Complete the sentences with the words below. There are four extra words.

> contraction enhancing famous known
> level rate reaching rhythm time

1 How fast should my heart _____ be?
2 Why can't athletics organisations stop people taking performance-_____ drugs?
3 Your bad diet may have far-_____ effects on your heart and liver.
4 I'll never be a top-_____ footballer.
5 It's well-_____ that he's a cheat.

/5

3 Comparatives Complete the sentences using the correct form of the words in brackets.

1 _____ (long) you wait before you go to the doctor, _____ (bad) you will feel.
2 _____ (healthy) you are, _____ (quick) your body will recover from illness.
3 _____ (good) the weather, _____ (happy) I feel.
4 _____ (expensive) medicine is, _____ (few) the people who can afford it.
5 _____ (old) I get, _____ (worried) I become about my health.

/5

4 Future Complete the sentences with *will + infinitive*, *will be + -ing* or *will have* + third form of the verb.

1 By the time I've finished my homework, it _____ (be) time for bed.
2 In an hour, the film _____ (finish) and the news will be on.
3 At nine o'clock this Saturday evening, I _____ (dance) with Steve at the disco.
4 I _____ (not forget) you when I'm famous.
5 By the end of the week, Tom _____ (see) this film four times. He loves it!

/5

5 Future Complete the sentences with one word in each gap.

1 There _____ _____ be several more outbreaks of the disease before it was brought under control.
2 I thought you _____ _____ _____ bring something to eat.
3 The president's healthcare ideas _____ cause him many problems in the years that followed.
4 When they arrived, the doctors were shocked at how bad the situation _____ .

/4

6 Linkers Complete the sentences with the correct answers.

1 We were late _____ of an accident.
  a due   b since   c because
2 He had a heart attack _____ to his bad diet.
  a due   b because   c in addition
3 _____ we weren't ill, we decided to ask the doctor to check our blood pressure.
  a Whereas   b Since   c Although
4 I am very health conscious _____ my brother doesn't worry about his health at all.
  a as   b whereas   c nevertheless
5 I have a very healthy lifestyle. _____ , I sometimes think I should be even more careful.
  a While   b Nevertheless   c Whereas

/5

TOTAL SCORE */30*

Module Diary

1 Look at the objectives on page 45 in the Students' Book. Choose three and evaluate your learning.

1 Now I can _____
  well / quite well / with problems.
2 Now I can _____
  well / quite well / with problems.
3 Now I can _____
  well / quite well / with problems.

2 Look at your results. What language areas in this module do you need to study more?

/5

Sound Choice 3

1 **1.33** Grammar - stress in passive constructions
Listen to the sentences and <u>underline</u> the part of the passive structure which is stressed. Listen again and repeat the sentences.

1 It's going to be <u>advertised</u> on TV.
2 It will only be sold online.
3 I'm not influenced by advertising.
4 Too much spam is sent every day.
5 Both his legs were broken.
6 The race was won in a record time.

2 **1.34** Consonants - /ð/, /θ/, /t/, /d/, /v/ and /f/ **Listen to the words and complete them with one of the letters or the pair of letters below.**

d f t th v

1 <u>th</u> en
2 fa __ er
3 __ at
4 li __ e
5 bir __
6 clo __ es
7 wor __
8 li __

3 **1.35** Consonants - /ð/, /θ/, /t/, /d/, /v/ and /f/ **Listen and number the words in the order you hear them.**

a there	4	tear	2	dare	1	fair	3
b than		fan		van		tan	
c taught		fought		thought			
d view		few		dew			
e fine		vine		dine			

4 **1.36** Vowels - /ei/, /eə/, /əu/, /au/, /iə/ and /uə/ **Write the words you hear next to the words with the same vowel sound.**

day	_play_	_____
there	_____	_____
go	_____	_____
now	_____	_____
hear	_____	_____
cure	_____	_____

5 **1.37** Spelling **Listen and complete each word with two vowels in each gap.**

1 rec _ei_ ve
2 n __ ghb __ r
3 pat __ nt
4 l __ gh
5 m __ sles
6 h __ lth
7 bel __ ve
8 w __ rd
9 n __ se
10 p __ n
11 c __ se
12 c __ gh

6 **1.38** Expressions - leaving out words **Listen to the dialogues. The first time, just listen. You will then hear A's part of the dialogue a second time. This time you should respond with B's part.**

1 **A:** That computer's expensive. **B:** How much?
2 **A:** My computer keeps freezing. **B:** Since when?
3 **A:** I saw Jane. **B:** When?
4 **A:** Mark won the race. **B:** He didn't!
5 **A:** Guess who I met. **B:** Who?
6 **A:** Let's meet here. **B:** What time?
7 **A:** My dad's got a new job. **B:** Has he?
8 **A:** I like Paul's new hairstyle. **B:** You don't!

7 **1.39** Difficult words - word stress in long words
Match the words below to the correct stress pattern. Then listen to check.

alternative celebrity diabetes diarrhoea
expectancy hepatitis intelligence meningitis
practitioner salmonella

oOoo	oOoo
conventional	constipation
_____	_____
_____	_____
_____	_____
_____	_____
_____	_____

TOPIC TALK - VOCABULARY

1 Match the people (1-9) with the adjectives (a-i).

1 Alan tends to forget things. _a_
2 When Cathy has an aim, she doesn't let anyone or anything stand in her way. ___
3 Asmir behaves unusually and differently to other people. ___
4 Lesley always wants to win. ___
5 Jeff isn't frightened of anyone. ___
6 Terry speaks clearly and is easy to understand even if the subject is difficult. ___
7 Rachel likes to be alone. ___
8 Sam behaves rudely because he thinks he's better than other people. ___
9 Michelle sometimes thinks and worries about things too much. ___

a absent-minded
b arrogant
c articulate
d competitive
e fearless
f eccentric
g reclusive
h determined
i obsessive

2 Choose the correct answers.

1 Lisa _a_ her nails.
  a bites   b shrugs   c taps
2 Neil ___ his mobile all the time.
  a fidgets   b blinks   c checks
3 Simon ___ his shoulders when he doesn't understand.
  a taps   b checks   c shrugs
4 Matt ___ his feet on the floor.
  a touches   b taps   c fidgets
5 Amanda ___ her hair all the time.
  a fidgets   b taps   c touches
6 My dad ___ when he is angry or confused.
  a frowns   b grins   c giggles
7 Look at Paul's eyes. He never ___ .
  a grins   b blinks   c frowns
8 I was ___ during the lesson because my friend told me a funny joke.
  a fidgeting   b frowning   c giggling

3 Complete the text with one word in each gap.

My best friend had a problem which he couldn't [1]s_olve_____ . I'm good at [2] a_____ problems so I helped him. I've got that sort of mind. That's why I enjoy [3]d_____ puzzles. I've got a lot of friends. I [4]g_____ on well with most people I know and I enjoy [5]w_____ with other people, for example when we are in groups in lessons. The only problem is that when I am in a group with my friends we spend all our time [6]t_____ each other jokes instead of doing what the teacher tells us to do.

Surprisingly, I'm a bit shy so I find it difficult to talk to strangers. My worst nightmare is to have to [7]m_____ a speech in front of a room full of people although I like [8]d_____ issues with my friends. I feel more comfortable with them.

4 Complete the text with the words below.

competitive   good   know   modest
playing   realise   ~~shy~~   sport   tends

This is Elaine. At first, she seems rather [1]___shy___ but, when you get to [2]_____ her, you [3]_____ that she's really quite self-confident. Sometimes, she [4]_____ to be slightly dreamy, especially during PE but usually she is pretty enthusiastic about what she is doing. She isn't at all [5]_____ and never cares about winning games or being the best in the class. Although she is very clever, she is also very [6]_____ and definitely not arrogant.

Elaine is [7]_____ at painting and drawing and [8]_____ the guitar but she can't sing and she isn't interested in playing [9]_____ .

REMEMBER

Complete Exercises A–B before you start this lesson.

A Complete the text with *a*, *an* or *the*.

I read [1] *a* great article about [2]___ boy who was [3]___ genius. When [4]___ boy was just eight years old, he painted [5]___ amazing picture. A year later he had [6]___ exhibition of his paintings. All [7]___ paintings at [8]___ exhibition were sold and he made a lot of money. Some people call him the new Picasso because Picasso also started painting at [9]___ same age but [10]___ boy prefers Degas. Although he's [11]___ genius, he is also [12]___ normal boy and he goes to [13]___ normal school. I read [14]___ article on [15]___ internet. I can't remember [16]___ address of the website now but I'll send you [17]___ email later and let you know what it is.

B Look at the information and complete the sentences with the words below.

~~all~~   most   no   none   some

Number of students in the school: 500
Number of students we talked to: 500
Number of students who like the school: 450
Number of students who worry about exams: 125
Number of students who would like to change schools: 0

1 ___*All*___ of the students answered the questions.
2 _____ of the students would like to change schools.
3 _____ of the students like the school.
4 _____ students want to change schools.
5 _____ of the students worry about their exams.

all   most   no   none   some

Number of blogs I've written: 20
Number of blogs which have earned money: 0
Number of blogs still online: 18
Number of blogs about music: 20
Number of blogs that got comments: 5

6 _____ of the blogs have earned money.
7 _____ of the blogs got comments.
8 _____ blogs were published in magazines.
9 _____ of the blogs were about music.
10 _____ of the blogs are still online.

1 * Match the reasons for their use (a–d) with the <u>underlined</u> articles.

a something unique
b something specific described in the same sentence
c something mentioned before
d one of many

1 Urbain-Jean-Joseph Le Verrier was <u>a</u> mathematician. _*d*_
2 He observed how Mercury moved around <u>the</u> sun. ___
3 He noticed that <u>the</u> planet's movement was strange. ___
4 Le Verrier thought that there might be <u>a</u> different planet near to Mercury which was affecting it. ___
5 He called it Vulcan after <u>the</u> Roman god of fire. ___
6 Other people claimed to have seen <u>the</u> planet. ___
7 However, after <u>the</u> death of Le Verrier, scientists began to doubt whether his theory was correct. ___
8 <u>The</u> search for the planet ended in 1915, which was also <u>the</u> year when Einstein's theory of relativity explained Mercury's movement. ___
9 Now Vulcan is most famous because of <u>a</u> character from the TV series, *Star Trek*. ___
10 Vulcan is <u>the</u> home of Mr Spock. ___

2 ** Complete the text with *a*, *an*, *the* or *-*.

Einstein is famous all over [1] _*the*_ world for his scientific theories but even he isn't right all the time. At that time, there was [2]_____ theory that said that [3]_____ universe had always been and would always be the same size. Einstein was one of [4]_____ theory's biggest supporters. In fact, [5]_____ theory, known as the static universe, is sometimes called [6]_____ Einstein's universe.

Since then, [7]_____ theory has been proved to be wrong. We can now see that stars and planets are moving away from us as [8]_____ universe gets bigger. Einstein realised he had made [9]_____ embarrassing error about the static universe. However, [10]_____ idea that [11]_____ universe is getting bigger is also just [12]_____ theory and there are still [13]_____ scientists who are trying to prove that this, too, is wrong.

3 ** Choose the correct words.**

I got two books out of the library. The first one was great but [1]another/other/~~the other~~ book was boring.

The Fermi Paradox states that there should be intelligent life on [2]another/other/the other planets but there is no evidence to prove it. That's why [3]another/other/the other scientist, Drake, has come up with a way of calculating the chances of finding life on [4]another/other/the other planet. The problem is that no one will know if he is right until someone finds that there definitely is or definitely isn't life anywhere else.

We learned about Newton's three laws at school. One was about the movement of an object and [5]another/other/the other was about the speed of an object. I can't remember what [6]another/other/the other one was about.

Charles Darwin is remembered in many ways. There's a Mount Darwin in the Andes. [7]Another/Other/The other place named after him is the town of Darwin in Australia. There are more places too but most of [8]another/other/the other things which have taken his name are plant and animal species.

4 *** Complete the text with the words below.**

a   all   ~~an~~   an   another   both   the (x 3)   this

Sir Francis Galton was Charles Darwin's cousin. He was [1] _an_ incredibly hard-working and intelligent man who published over 340 papers and books during his life. He thought of [2]_____ phrase 'nature versus nurture'. [3]_____ phrase looks at the question of how much of [4]_____ person's character and intelligence they are born with and how much is learned. He was also [5]_____ investigator of [6]_____ human mind and he is often called [7]_____ father of psychometrics, the science of studying mental ability. [8]_____ thing he thought of was the first ever weather map and he also invented a type of whistle to test people's hearing ability.

His interest in science and evolution started when he read Darwin's *On the Origin of Species*. [9]_____ he and Darwin made incredible discoveries but Galton took Darwin's work much further. Not [10]_____ of his theories and ideas are still believed today but many of them are and he deserves to be as famous as his well-known cousin.

Grammar Alive
Talking about more than one person

5 *** Complete the dialogues from the cues.**

1 / Alexander Graham Bell / really invent / telephone?
Well, / Bell and / scientist / Gray / had / same idea / same time
/ scientists / trying to invent / telephone / that time?
Yes, / lots – for example / Manzetti, Meucci, Reis, Edison

Did Alexander Graham Bell really invent the telephone?
Well, Bell and another scientist, Gray, had the same idea at the same time.

_____

_____

2 Who / Brahmagupta / Bhaskaracharya and where / come from?
/ Indian mathematicians
/ live / same time?
No – live 7th century / live 12th century
How / similar / each other?
/ wrote about gravity several hundred years before Newton

_____

_____

_____

_____

_____

_____

1 Read the text quickly and match Dupin (D) and the sailor (S) with the correct list of adjectives (1-4). There are two extra lists of adjectives.

1 dangerous, sinister, evil, violent

2 frightened, harmless, nervous, honest

3 calm, thoughtful, careful, prepared

4 arrogant, eccentric, curious, brave

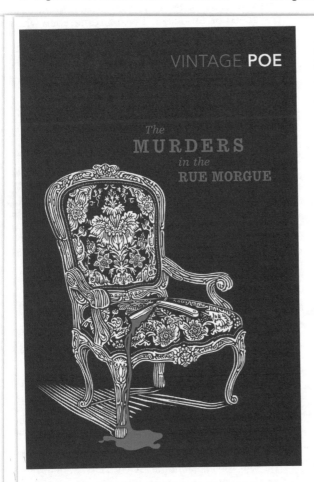

VINTAGE **POE**

The
MURDERS
in the
RUE MORGUE

At this moment we heard a step upon the stairs.

'Be ready,' said Dupin, 'with your pistols, but neither use them nor show them until at a signal from myself.'

The front door of the house had been left open, and the visitor had entered, without ringing, and advanced several steps upon the staircase. Now, however, he seemed to hesitate and he went down again. Dupin moved quickly to the door when we heard him coming up once more. The visitor did not turn back a second time, but stepped up with decision, and knocked at the door of our room.

'Come in,' said Dupin, in a cheerful voice.

A man entered. He was a sailor, a tall, muscular-looking person. His face, greatly sunburnt, was more than half hidden by beard and moustache.

'Sit down, my friend,' said Dupin. 'I suppose you have called about the orangutang. A remarkably fine, and no doubt a very valuable animal.'

The sailor breathed heavily.

'Have you got him here?' he inquired.

'Oh no. You can get him in the morning. Of course you are prepared to identify him?'

'To be sure I am, sir.'

'I shall be sorry to part with him,' said Dupin.

'I don't mean that you should have all this trouble for nothing, sir,' said the man. 'I'm very willing to pay a reward for finding the animal.'

'Well,' replied my friend, 'that is all very fair, to be sure. Let me think! What should I have? Oh! I will tell you. My reward for finding him shall be this. You shall give me all the information in your power about these murders in the Rue Morgue.'

Dupin whispered the last words very quietly. Just as quietly, too, he strode toward the door, locked it, and put the key in his pocket. He then drew a pistol from his jacket and placed it, calmly, upon the table.

The sailor stared at Dupin, his face went red and he fell back into his seat, shaking violently. He spoke not a word.

'My friend,' said Dupin, in a kind tone, 'you are alarming yourself unnecessarily. We mean you no harm whatever. I promise that we intend you no injury. I perfectly well know that you are innocent of the murders. You have nothing to hide. On the other hand, you must confess all you know. An innocent man is now imprisoned, charged with that crime and you know who really did it. By telling us the truth, you can help to free him.'

'So help me God,' said the sailor, after a brief pause, 'I will tell you all I know, but I do not expect you to believe one half of it. Still, I am innocent, and I will tell all, even if I die for it.'

EDGAR ALLAN POE *The MURDERS in the RUE MORGUE*

2 Read the texts again and choose the correct answers.

1 Before the sailor came into the room, Dupin:
   a had no idea who was coming.
   b thought there might be a chance of danger.
   c went outside to look for him.
   d wasn't expecting anyone to visit him.

2 When the sailor first arrived, he:
   a went straight up the stairs to the room.
   b climbed some of the way, stopped and then continued to the room.
   c went up some of the way, went down again and then went up to the room.
   d came up as far as the room, then went downstairs before coming up again.

3 From the text, it is impossible to say anything about the sailor's:
   a complexion.
   b build.
   c hair.
   d height.

4 From the text we can understand that Dupin:
   a had probably put out a notice saying that he had caught an orangutang.
   b had read about the orangutang but didn't know where it was.
   c had heard about the orangutang but not seen it.
   d didn't believe that the orangutang belonged to the man.

5 When Dupin mentioned the murders, he:
   a threatened the man with his gun.
   b made sure the man couldn't escape.
   c held the gun in his hand all the time.
   d talked in the same tone of voice all the time.

6 According to Dupin, the sailor:
   a was responsible for the murders.
   b was in danger because of the murders.
   c had helped to put an innocent man in prison.
   d knew something about the murders.

Word Builder Word families

3 Complete the words with one letter in each gap.

Say/Speak
1 e x c l a i m
2 s _ _ r _
3 w _ _ s p _ _

Ask
4 b _ _
5 i _ q _ _ _ e

Look at
6 o _ _ _ r v _
7 s _ _ r _ a t

Walk
8 s _ _ _ d _
9 s _ r _ l _
10 t _ _ t _ _

4 Complete the sentences with the correct form of the words from Exercise 3.

1 'He's got a gun,' she _exclaimed_ in frightened voice.
2 He _____ at the picture on the wall for several minutes.
3 Mark _____ quickly into the office.
4 'Please, please don't hurt me,' he _____ .
5 The police officer said that he had _____ the criminal coming out of the bank at 5.30 a.m.
6 Would you like to _____ around the park with me?
7 'Don't move or I'll shoot,' he _____ angrily.
8 'Who are you?' she _____ suspiciously.
9 We took our boots off and _____ into the room as quietly as we could.
10 'Don't make a sound,' she _____ quietly.

Sentence Builder by/for + -ing

5 Complete the sentences with by or for and the correct form of the verb in brackets.

1 The police found the body _by using_ (use) specially trained dogs.
2 He was sent to prison _____ (steal) $1 million.
3 The criminals made plans _____ (sell) the paintings they had stolen.
4 We worked out his plans _____ (observe) him carefully for several weeks.
5 We knew who the gang members were _____ (listen) to the leader's telephone conversations.
6 The police officers thanked us _____ (help) them.
7 The detective gave his men instructions _____ (catch) the thieves without any violence.
8 I found the information I needed _____ (ask) the right questions.

23

Oral Skills

Listening

1 **1.40** Listen to seven answers (1-7) from an interview about the BRIT school for performing arts and technology. Match them with the questions (a-h). There is one extra question.

a How can I find out more about the school? ___

b Is it expensive to study there? ___

c How does the school help the local community? ___

d How can I get into the school? ___

e What facilities does the school have? ___

f How is life there different to a normal school? _1_

g How did the school start? ___

h What sort of jobs do they train you for? ___

2 **1.40** Listen again to the first two answers from the interview. Complete the notes below.

1 a Ages of students: _14-19_

   b What students want: _____

   c How the school is different to other schools:

     _____

2 a Where students live: _____

   b Exceptions: _____

   c What they want to hear from potential students in the interview:

     _____

Sentence Builder Emphasis (3)

3 Complete the sentences with *do*, *does* or *did*.

1 It's not all fun and games - they _do_ study for exams, too!

2 It _____ cost a lot to pay for everything.

3 The school _____ need a lot of help to be able to start.

4 We _____ need to ask students to pay for some things.

5 The school _____ help students a lot.

6 My mum _____ have a few worries before she went to the open day.

4 Complete the replies with *do*, *does* or *did* in the correct place.

1 **A:** I'm sorry you weren't successful. Next time, I hope you will try harder.

   B: I _did_ try hard but it was very difficult.

2 **A:** I don't think you're serious about your studies.

   B: I am. I ___ want to succeed, really.

3 **A:** Your son isn't very happy here.

   B: He ___ like the school but he ___ have problems with some of the other students.

Speaking

1 **1.41** Complete the dialogues with one word in each gap. Then listen to check your answers.

1 **A:** Right, we had ten applications for places at our school and four of them were no good at all.

   B: So, that [1]_means_ there are six people to interview, [2]r_____ ?

   A: Exactly.

2 **A:** Thank you for coming to this interview. We'd like you to tell us your personal vision.

   B: Er … what do you mean [3]b_____ that, [4]e_____ ?

   A: Okay. Well, to [5]p_____ it another [6]w_____ , how do you see your future career?

3 **A:** Thank you for coming. You've applied for our theatre group and I can see you have been in several school productions. In other [7]w_____ , you must really enjoy acting.

   B: Yes I do, but I've also written a couple of plays so I'm keen to learn about directing, too.

4 **A:** So, that's the end of the interview. Just to [8]r_____ , you're hoping to get onto our broadcasting media course, is that right?

   B: Yes, I'd love to work as a television producer.

5 **A:** So, who do you think we should take?

   B: Well, [9]a_____ I said before, they are all excellent. I think we should think about changing our entrance policy.

   A: I don't quite [10]g_____ that.

   B: [11]W_____ I mean to [12]s_____ is, let's take four people, not just one.

2 Make sentences from the cues.

1 **A:** We believe in artistic freedom.

   B: / other / you / not like / be told what to do

     In other words, you don't like being told what

     to do.

2 **A:** I write hundreds of songs every day.

   B: As / said / you should think of quality not quantity

     _____

3 **A:** We are a futuristic blues rock theatrical experience.

   B: Sorry / not / quite get. Could / explain / mean / ?

     _____

4 **A:** Paul loves all kinds of music and can play five instruments.

   B: put / way / he / very musical!

     _____

24 GRAMMAR
Uncertainty

1 * **Complete the sentences with the correct form of the words in brackets.**

1 My friends _tend to waste_ (tend / waste) a lot of time playing computer games.

2 The test we did last week _____ (be supposed / be) easy.

3 You've all done so much work this year, you _____ (be bound / pass) your exams.

4 Success often _____ (seem / depend) on how rich a person's parents are.

5 Education _____ (be supposed / be) better in the past.

6 Summers _____ (seem / go) on forever when I was young.

7 People _____ (tend / assume) that I am unintelligent because of my clothes.

8 This year's group _____ (be supposed / be) the best in the school.

9 Students _____ (tend / become) lazier when the sun comes out.

2 ** **Choose the correct words.**

1 It's a nice day. I'll _a_ go for a cycle ride later.
   a probably   **b** may   **c** clearly

2 I can't go out today but ___ I'll have time tomorrow. I don't know yet.
   a obviously   **b** perhaps   **c** definitely

3 Leo ___ be on the plane by now. It was supposed to leave at 3.30 and it's nearly four now.
   a probably   **b** must   **c** obviously

4 I thought I saw Tina in the town centre but it ___ her because she's on holiday.
   a can't be   **b** probably isn't
   c can't have been

5 Our taxi driver has gone round in a circle. He ___ doesn't know where he's going.
   a perhaps   **b** obviously   **c** must

6 You ___ pass your driving test if you don't look in your mirror.
   a will probably **b** may not have
   c definitely won't

7 I ___ a summer job this year. I'm going to be away for most of the time.
   a probably won't get
   b may get
   c can't have got

8 I must phone my parents. They ___ heard about the bomb in the High Street yet.
   a may not have   **b** probably won't
   c definitely didn't

3 ** **Complete the sentences with the correct form of the words below.**

can't / see   definitely / set up   may / come
bound / give   probably / not get   ~~must / arrive~~
probably / be   must / read

1 Nigel's train _must have arrived_ by now. I wonder where he is.

2 Tom _____ and see us later.

3 I _____ a part in the school play. I'm not good enough.

4 You _____ this film yet. This is the first day it's been on.

5 Mr Davies _____ us a test tomorrow. We haven't had one for ages.

6 Your mum _____ your report by now. I wonder what she thinks about it.

7 There _____ an exercise on future tenses in the exam tomorrow.

8 Steve _____ his own business when he leaves university.

4 *** **Complete the second sentence so that it has the same meaning as the first. Use the word in capitals.**

I'm sure you'll do well at university.

1 (BOUND)
   You're _____ bound to do well at university._

2 (DEFINITELY)
   You _____

3 (CERTAINLY)
   You _____

There's a good chance that his invention will work.

4 (PROBABLY)
   His _____

There isn't much chance of our band being successful.

5 (PROBABLY)
   Our _____

I'm convinced that Harry didn't write this himself.

6 (CAN'T)
   Harry _____

7 (OBVIOUSLY)
   Harry _____

8 (DEFINITELY)
   Harry _____

Writing Workshop 6

1 Look at the description of the person in Exercise 2 and complete the words 1–17.

Appearance

¹d*ark* , *large* , *eyes*
²g_____ s_____
³l_____ , b_____ , w_____ h_____

Personality

⁴e_____   ⁵l_____
⁶s_____ sensitive
⁷a_____-m _____
⁸s_____-m _____
⁹d_____

Habits/Behaviour

¹⁰loves being the c_____ of a_____
¹¹f_____ m_____

Clothes

¹²s_____   ¹³b_____
¹⁴never j_____
¹⁵e_____ d_____

Opinions

¹⁶w_____   ¹⁷slightly a_____

2 Read the description again and complete it with the words below.

> dressing   faults   looks   ~~notice~~   realise
> seems   strikes   tends

The first thing you ¹ _notice_ about Jaqui is her eyes. They are dark and very large. The next thing that ²_____ you about her is her gorgeous smile and her long, blonde, wavy hair. She is eighteen but she ³_____ about twenty-two.

When you first meet Jaqui, she ⁴_____ a bit too excitable and lively but if you get to know her, you ⁵_____ that she has a serious, sensitive side to her character, too. When she is in a crowd, though, she loves being the centre of attention.

Of course, Jaqui has her ⁶_____ . She is quite absent-minded and ⁷_____ to forget meetings which she has arranged with her friends. At school, she is completely the opposite. She is very single-minded and determined and it is clear that she is going to be a successful businesswoman one day. Jaqui likes to look good and loves buying clothes and ⁸_____ up. She usually wears skirts and blouses. She sometimes wears trousers but never jeans and, when she goes out on a date, she always puts on elegant dresses.

To sum up, Jaqui is a wonderful, although slightly annoying, friend. She makes you feel really special when you are alone with her but don't expect her to look after you at a party because she won't have time!

3 Complete the questions with the words in Exercise 2. You may have to change the form of some of the words.

1 What's the first thing you __*notice*__ about him/her?
2 What else _____ you about his/her appearance?
3 Does he/she _____ older or younger than his/her real age?
4 How does he/she _____ when you first meet him/her?
5 What do you _____ about his/her character when you get to know him/her better?
6 What are his/her main _____ ? Are they very annoying?
7 Does he/she like _____ up or does he/she prefer to wear old, comfortable clothes?

4 Use the cues to make sentences and add extra information in a relative clause.

1 spiky / red / hair / shaved at the sides / strange-looking
   Strange-looking spiky, red hair which is shaved at the sides.
2 brown / eyes / small / usually red because he uses his computer too much
   _____
3 / arms / covered in tattoos /muscular / strong /
   _____
4 old / torn / jeans / black / very tight
   _____

5 Use your imagination to write about <u>one</u> of the two people in the pictures. Include the information below.

17 years old, intelligent, shy, loyal friend   35 years old, adventurous, sporty, talkative, fun-loving

- The first thing you notice when you see him/her.
- What you first think about his/her character and what you later realise.
- His/Her real character and habits.
- How he/she likes to dress.
- Your feelings about him/her.

Write between 120 and 180 words.

Check Your Progress 6

❶ Personality Complete the text with the correct form of the words in brackets.

Annabel is my best friend at school. She is very
¹_____ (AMBITION) and determined but
she can also be a bit ²_____ (DREAM) at
times. She's got a great sense of humour and is very
³_____ (WIT).
She loves sports. She is very ⁴_____
(COMPETE) and ⁵_____ (ENTHUSIAST)
about whatever she is doing.
Annabel is a good student. She is ⁶_____
(LOGIC) so she is good at maths and sciences and
she is also ⁷_____ (CREATE) so is good
at art and music. She works hard but she isn't too
⁸_____ (DRIVE). She knows how to enjoy
herself, too.

/8

❷ Reference Choose the correct answers.

1 My cousin and I are very similar. We are *all/each/
both* very absent-minded.
2 I've got three computer games. Two of them are
on my desk but I don't know where *another/other/
the other* one is.
3 Do you want to see my holiday photos? *This/The
other/The* one is of me in Paris.
4 I've got *the/an/a* important exam next week.
5 We've had two exams today and we've got
another/other/the other one tomorrow.
6 Our teacher is late for the lesson. He's probably in
a/the/this staff room.

/6

❸ Word families Complete the sentences with the correct form of the words below.

> beg   inquire   observe   snarl   stare   stride

1 I _____ at the wall for several minutes and
then started writing
2 She _____ us to help her but there was
nothing we could do.
3 We knocked on the door. A man answered. 'Go
away!' he _____ nastily.
4 I _____ about my lost wallet but no one in the
café had seen it.
5 You can learn a lot about people by _____
them carefully for a few days.
6 Our teacher always _____ determinedly and
quickly into the classroom.

/6

❹ *by/for* + *-ing* Complete the sentences with *by* or *for* and the correct form of the verb in brackets.

1 They got into the house (climb) _____
through a bedroom window.
2 I won a prize (have) _____ the best
exam results in my year.
3 My mum told me off (not wear) _____
a coat to school.
4 You can help us (phone) _____ your
local police station with information.

/4

❺ Uncertainty Make sentences from the cues.

A: Oh no! There are no more tickets for the concert.
B: They / can't / sell them all yet
¹_____

A: Paul / supposed / buy / some last week but he
forgot.
²_____
_____

B: He / tend / forget / most things he promises to do.
³_____

A: I / definitely / not / ask him to do anything
important in the future.
⁴_____
_____

B: Don't worry. There / bound / be / some for sale on
the internet.
⁵_____
_____

A: Yes but they / probably / not / be cheap
⁶_____

/6

TOTAL SCORE **/30**

Module Diary

❶ Look at the objectives on page 55 in the Students' Book. Choose three and evaluate your learning.

1 Now I can _____
well / quite well / with problems.
2 Now I can _____
well / quite well / with problems.
3 Now I can _____
well / quite well / with problems.

❷ Look at your results. What language areas in this module do you need to study more?

Exam Choice 3

Reading

1 Read the text quickly and decide on the best title.

A Healthy eating habits that modern humans have forgotten.

B Problems faced by people following the Stone Age diet.

C Improving the health of the Kitava tribe by changing their diet.

Staffan Lindeberg is a professor in the department of medicine at the University of Lund in Sweden. He trained in family medicine and became interested in the effects of diets on our well-being. He was especially interested in a Stone Age diet, that is, the food people ate many thousands of years ago before humans started farming. In the early 1990s he travelled to Papua New Guinea to study the diet of the people on the island of Kitava as this was very close to the Stone Age diet. While there, he found that the people did not suffer from strokes, heart attacks, diabetes, being overweight and many other diseases common in western countries.

As a result of his findings, he decided to test patients in Sweden to see how such a diet would affect them. Fourteen patients followed a Stone Age diet while another fifteen followed a Mediterranean diet, also healthy with lots of fruit and vegetables. All of the patients in the tests had high blood sugar levels, most suffered from diabetes and they all had some problems with their hearts.

At the end of three months, the group following the Mediterranean diet had reduced their blood sugar levels by a small amount but those following the Stone Age diet had much lower levels of sugar in their blood. The patients in both groups also lost weight although the level of sugar in the blood and the patients' weight didn't seem to be related.

So, what is it about the Stone Age diet that can make us more healthy? The diet contains some meat, fish, fruit, vegetables and nuts but it doesn't contain any dairy products or grains, such as wheat or rice, and there is no salt.

The next question is whether the Kitava people are more healthy than us. After all, their life expectancy is much lower. According to Professor Lindeberg, this is not as simple as we may think. Because of their lack of healthcare, there is more chance of them dying at a young age. However, if people on Kitava manage to reach fifty, they tend to live as long as people in more developed countries.

A final question that people often ask is whether our bodies have now adapted to eating grain and dairy food as we have been eating them for so long. According to Darwin's theory of evolution, species, including humans, change over time so, what was unhealthy for us thousands of years ago, may now be healthy!

2 Read the text again. Decide whether the sentences are true (T), false (F) or there is no information (NI).

1 Staffan Lindeberg believes that the Stone Age diet is the healthiest that people can follow. ___
2 The tests in Sweden compared fourteen healthy people with fifteen unhealthy people. ___
3 Both the diets used in the tests were healthy. ___
4 There is a close relationship between blood sugar levels and weight. ___
5 The Kitava diet is a vegetarian one. ___
6 People on Kitava have the same life expectancy as Stone Age people had. ___
7 There is no one on Kitava who is over fifty years old. ___
8 Our bodies cannot adapt to a grain and dairy food diet because Darwin's theory of evolution doesn't work for humans. ___

Listening

3 **1.42** Listen to a woman talking about a comedian. Complete the notes.

1 Date of birth:
16th June _____
2 Real name:
Arthur _____
3 1910 toured:
_____
4 Weekly earnings as a silent film actor:
_____
5 What he wanted to do instead of acting:
work as a _____
6 A film that looks at the change from silent films to 'talkies':
_____
7 Reasons for Laurel and Hardy's career coming to an end:
war, age and _____
8 Health problem they both had in the 1950s:
_____
9 How he spent a lot of time in his retirement:
_____
10 The last thing he said he'd like to do:
_____

Speaking

4 Complete the dialogue with one word in each gap.

Examiner: I'd now like you to discuss the changes you think people should make to their lives to be more healthy.

Student 1: Well, in my [1]o _____ , the first thing they should do is to change their diet. In western countries, people eat too much fat and too much salt. [2]B _____ of that, we suffer from heart attacks, strokes and other health problems.

Student 2: A lot of people are overweight, too. The main [3]r _____ for that is that they eat too much.

Student 1: But it's also because of their lifestyles.

Student 2: What do you [4]m _____ by that, exactly?

Student 1: Stress. The [5]f _____ is that our lives are too busy and hurried. Even when people eat healthy food, they don't sit down and relax, they eat at their computers or while walking along the street. And we are too sedentary.

Student 2: I'm sorry, I don't know that word.

Student 1: Well, to [6]p _____ it another [7]w _____ , we don't get enough exercise and we spend too much time sitting. I've read that it's better to be overweight but get exercise than to be thin but not do anything.

Student 2: Really? So thin lazy people are more likely to get ill than active overweight people, is that [8]r _____ ?

Student 1: Exactly. So, to [9]r _____ , we believe that the changes people need to make are to eat more healthily, be more relaxed and get more exercise.

Examiner: Thank you.

Exam Choice 3

Use of English

5 Complete the text with one word in each gap.

My brother is good at sciences. In fact, I'd say he was ^{1}_____ genius. I'm not as clever as him but we ^{2}_____ like the same subjects. He's older than me. He's twenty now. Last year, he ^{3}_____ going to start university but, in the end, he decided to take a year off. ^{4}_____ course he wants to study costs about £9000 a year. He ^{5}_____ have some money in the bank but he wants to have more before he starts the course. So, he's working in a factory and, by the end of the year, he will ^{6}_____ saved about £6000. He also earns money ^{7}_____ giving private science lessons to school students who are worried about their exams. He's got three students who come for help regularly and they ^{8}_____

say that he's a great teacher. At one stage, he ^{9}_____ think about becoming a teacher but I think he's changed his mind now. Whatever he decides to do, he's bound ^{10}_____ be good at it. He always is.

Writing

6 Choose the correct linking words.

1 Children are just as interested in sport as they have always been. ___ , they don't get as much exercise as children in the past.
   a While   **b** Nevertheless   **c** Since

2 ___ of computers and other things to do, children don't spend as much time playing outside.
   a Since   **b** Due   **c** As a result

3 ___ there are more sports clubs and gyms, there are fewer parks and open spaces.
   a While   **b** However   **c** As

4 Most children enjoy playing in the street. ___ , parents are often afraid to let them out alone.
   a Since   **b** Although   **c** However

5 It is actually safer for children to go cycling nowadays ___ there are so many special bike paths for them to use.
   a although   **b** because   **c** due to

6 It's probably true that young people don't get as much exercise as they used to, ___ I don't believe the problem is as bad as some people think.
   a whereas   **b** although   **c** as

7 Write an opinion essay on the topic below. Use some of the ideas in Exercise 6 if you want to.

Young people these days don't get enough exercise.

Write between 120 and 180 words.

TOPIC TALK – VOCABULARY

1 Complete the words in the puzzle using the clues below.

¹c	l	u	b	s				
²	o							
³	m							
⁴	m							
⁵	u							
⁶	n							
⁷	i							
⁸	t							
⁹	y							

1 Places where people can go and meet each other.
2 Places where sick people get better.
3 Things which are against the law.
4 The problem of people not having work.
5 ___ transport includes buses and trains.
6 Special things that happen such as concerts or festivals.
7 Places where you can go to borrow books.
8 Rubbish thrown onto the ground.
9 Places for children to go and have fun.

2 Complete the words with one letter in each gap.

It's unfriendly here.
1 People keep to t _h_ e m _s_ e l _v_ e s.
2 Nobody knows their n _ _ g _ b _ _ _ s.
3 People are n _ _ y and want to know what you are doing.
There is a lot of poverty.
4 You see people b _ _ g _ _ _ in the streets.
5 There is a lot of h _ _ _ l _ s _ n _ _ s.
6 There are a lot of b _ _ r _ _ d-up shops.
There are a lot of social problems.
7 There is p _ _ l _ _ d _ _ _ k _ _ _ .
8 There are quite a few b _ _ g _ _ r _ _ _ .
9 There is a lot of v _ _ d _ l _ _ _ .
It's bad for our health.
10 There is a lot of p _ l _ _ t _ _ _ .
11 There is very h _ _ v _ t _ _ f _ _ _ on the streets.
12 There is a lack of decent s _ n _ _ _ t _ _ n.

3 Complete the text with one word in each gap.

Votes for Teenagers Campaign

We want to take ¹__part__ in making local ²d_____ . The local ³c_____ should listen to us as well as to older people and the only way they are going to do that is if we could vote in local ⁴e_____ from the age of sixteen.

If we could vote, we would demand more free ⁵a_____ for teenagers to take part in, more local ⁶c_____ for us to go to and other places we could ⁷h_____ out in and have fun. At the moment, we have to meet in the park or the street where there is no ⁸p_____ from nosy people. It's not right. It's great that people help each other ⁹o_____ with their problems and that the streets are ¹⁰s_____ at night but, sometimes we'd like to be with our friends.

Join our campaign today!

4 Complete the text with the words below.

abandoned   accidents   best   better   gangs
graffiti   ~~know~~   lack   lock   own   trust

I've lived in my hometown all my life and I ¹__know__ a lot of people. The ²_____ thing about living here is that the people are friendly and you don't need to ³_____ your front door when you go out. Dad often leaves the car open all night and it's always there in the morning. You can ⁴_____ people and children can go out on their ⁵_____ , even after dark.
The worst thing about the area is that it's boring. There is a ⁶_____ of green spaces and no clubs or anything for teenagers. It would be ⁷_____ for young people if we had more places to go to. There's quite a lot of ⁸_____ on the walls of buildings because teenagers are bored. Luckily, it's quite a rich area and there aren't any street ⁹_____ or serious crimes. There was an ¹⁰_____ car once. It was there for a week and then the police took it away. I don't think they ever found the owner. There have been quite a few traffic ¹¹_____ recently, too. I think it's because my brother has just started taking driving lessons!

1 Look at the photos and guess the correct answers. Then read the text quickly to check.

1 The tribe is from *South America/Asia/Africa*.

2 At their festivals they do a lot of singing and *dancing/fighting/eating*.

2 They are famous for their *hairstyles/jewellery/ brightly coloured clothes*.

The Lisu Hill tribe originally came from Tibet. They left their homeland about three hundred years ago and there are now Lisu Hill people in Burma, India, Laos, China and in northern Thailand. In 1921, four families set up a village in northern Thailand and today there are about 55,000 members of the tribe living in the area.

For many years, the tribe lived by agriculture. They used a method known as 'swidden'. This means that they cut down an area of rainforest and used the land to farm. When all the goodness in the ground had been used up, they moved on and cut down another area of the forest. This method of farming can be very dangerous for the environment if the forest is cut down too quickly. It may never grow again. However, with a small group, like the Lisu people, the forest does have time to regrow and the same land can be used again in the future. But today the Lisu are not the only people in the area. Roads are being built, the forest is being cut down and other people are moving into the area.

That's why the Lisu people have had to find new ways to survive, one of which is the village homestay idea. Small numbers of tourists can stay in the Lisu villages overnight to experience for themselves how the tribe lives. They can join in with activities such as picking fruit and herbs or helping to cook the evening meal. Alternatively they can just hang around and observe the villagers getting on with their lives. If they are lucky, the tourists may arrive at the time of a wedding or a festival with its music, dancing and traditional song. Singing is very important to the Lisu people as, traditionally, they had no written language and the tribe's history was passed from generation to generation through song. They are now able to write words using the western alphabet to represent the sounds of their language.

A village homestay is not only a unique and rewarding experience for a tourist but is also important for the tribe. Firstly, the money the visitors pay helps them to buy food and other necessities, especially if the tourists buy some of their handmade crafts, such as their beautiful necklaces, as well. Secondly, they show the tribe that the outside world is interested in them and their culture which helps to make them even more proud of what they are. In addition, knowing that visitors are only visiting them to experience their traditional culture, they are less likely to try to change their way of life.

The Lisu Hill tribe are a fascinating, friendly group of people. Why not visit them yourself?

2 Read the text again and choose the correct answers.

1 The Lisu Hill tribe now live:
   a in Thailand only.
   b in several different countries including their original homeland.
   c in several different countries but not their original homeland.
   d altogether in one village.

2 The farming method 'swidden':
   a can never be environmentally friendly.
   b still works for the Lisu tribe.
   c would work if the Lisu were left alone.
   d isn't necessary any longer because of improvements in agriculture.

3 The village homestay idea started up because the tribe:
   a wanted extra money.
   b needed help with their work.
   c like company.
   d wanted to learn English.

4 The tribe traditionally:
   a didn't write stories down.
   b had their own alphabet which is now lost.
   c hold special festivals for their visitors.
   d used the same alphabet as western countries.

5 Which of these is not mentioned in the text as a reason why the village homestay idea is a good one?
   a It earns the tribe money.
   b It helps them to learn English.
   c It makes them keep their traditions.
   d It gives the villagers a sense of pride in their culture.

6 The best title for the text would be:
   a A history of the Lisu Hill tribe.
   b My life with the Lisu Hill tribe.
   c A fascinating tribe to visit.
   d A tribe in danger from the modern world.

Word Builder Multi-part verbs (3)

3 Complete the sentences with the correct form of the verbs below.

be not be come get (x2)
hang head set stack

1 At last, we _were_ off.
2 The women _____ on with the cooking and cleaning while the men hunted for animals.
3 We have been travelling through the rainforest for ten hours but our journey _____ over yet.
4 Do you want to _____ on to the village while we wait here for the others?
5 Before we leave, the tents have to _____ down.
6 The other van will be late because it has _____ stuck in the mud.
7 How long will it take to _____ up this equipment? We need to start using it immediately.
8 These tents need to be carefully _____ away.
9 There are always a few bullies _____ around the shopping centre and making comments about our clothes.

Sentence Builder Verbs of perception + infinitive/-ing form

4 Complete the sentences using the cues.

Yesterday, in the cinema these things were happening while I was watching the film.
1 I hear / someone's phone / ring
   I heard someone's phone ringing.
2 I see / man / video / the film
   _____
3 I watch / two girls / argue
   _____

This morning before I went to school, these things happened.
4 I listen / my brother / tell a joke
   I listened to my brother tell a joke.

5 watch / my dad / try / make a fried egg
   _____

6 hear / the newsreader on the radio / report on last night's football results.
   _____
   _____

71

26

Conditionals

REMEMBER

Complete Exercises A–B before you start this lesson.

A Match the beginnings (1–9) with the correct endings (a–i).

1 If I lived in a big city, _h_
2 If I hadn't hurt my leg last week, ___
3 If you're late again, ___
4 I'd be sad ___
5 I won't tell anyone your secret ___
6 I'd have won the race ___
7 Would you have invited me to your party ___
8 Will you go to the park tomorrow ___
9 Would you live in a big city ___

a I'll be annoyed.
b if the party hadn't been just for close family?
c if I didn't have any friends.
d if you don't want me to.
e if the weather is nice?
f I'd have played football.
g if you could?
h I'd be scared.
i if I had worn my lucky trainers.

B Choose the correct form.

1 If I *don't have/didn't have* a bike, I'd go to school by bus.
2 If I *didn't have/hadn't had* an exam the next day, I'd have gone out last Sunday.
3 Will you stay in this town if you *don't go/didn't go* to university?
4 *Would you say/Will you say* anything if you saw someone dropping litter?
5 If you go out with your friends later, where *will you meet/would you meet* them?
6 *Would you be/Would you have been* upset last week if I hadn't phoned you?

1 * Complete the sentences with the phrases below.

I wouldn't have met   I wouldn't leave
there would have been   there wouldn't be
they would be   they wouldn't have moved
~~would it be~~   you could have taken

1 If men had babies, _____would it be_____ their job to stay at home and look after them?
2 If the playground hadn't been vandalised, _____ your young cousins there yesterday.
3 If they hadn't opened a new road around the town, _____ more accidents in the town centre.
4 If sixteen-year-olds could vote, _____ more interested in politics.
5 If there were more things for teenagers to do here, _____ so much vandalism.
6 If I hadn't joined the youth club last year, _____ Kate.
7 If I didn't trust my neighbours in the village, _____ my door unlocked.
8 If my parents had known about the crime in this area, _____ here.

2 ** Complete the sentences with the correct form of the verbs in brackets.

1 If there hadn't been a riot last week, there _____wouldn't be_____ (not be) so many burnt-out buildings today.
2 If my mum earned more money, then my dad _____ (stay) at home.
3 If there had been a football club in my town, I _____ (join) it.
4 If the council had built more houses, fewer people _____ (be) homeless now.
5 Our parents would let us stay out after dark if they _____ (not be) so worried.
6 My parents _____ (not know) about my party if our neighbours weren't so nosy.
7 The burglars _____ (take) dad's laptop last week if they had noticed it.
8 If our council cared more about teenagers, they _____ (organise) more activities for them last summer.
9 If our neighbours _____ (tell) us that they were having problems last year, we would have tried to help them.
10 If the pollution _____ (not be) so bad, we could sit outside in the garden.

3 ** Complete the sentences with the correct form of the verbs in brackets.**

If I had passed my exams, my parents:

1 _____wouldn't be_____ (not be) angry with me now.

2 _____ (not be) angry with me last year.

If I hadn't dropped litter on the ground last week:

3 the police _____ (not stop) me.

4 I _____ (have) more money to spend on clothes now.

If I had practised the guitar when I was younger:

5 Mark _____ (ask) me to join his band last year.

6 I _____ (be) a star at my school now.

If our neighbours were friendly:

7 this _____ (be) a nicer place to live.

8 we _____ (invite) them to our barbecue last Sunday.

If buses were cheaper:

9 I _____ (can afford) to use them more often.

10 I _____ (not cycle) into town last Saturday.

4 *** Complete the sentences to make imaginary situations and results.**

1 My dad was in a hurry – he had an accident – he's in hospital now

If my dad ___hadn't been in a hurry___ , he ___wouldn't have had___ an accident.

If he _____hadn't had_____ an accident, he _____wouldn't be_____ in hospital now.

2 A new factory opened – the air became polluted – old people often get sick now

If the factory _____ , the air _____ polluted.

If the air _____ polluted, old people _____ so often now.

3 I played football in the garden – I broke the neighbour's window – I don't get any pocket money now

If I _____ in the garden, I _____ the neighbour's window.

If I _____ the neighbour's window, I _____ pocket money now.

5 *** Answer the questions using the cues.**

What would the situation be now if your parents had moved to a different town last year?

1 (go / different / school)
  I would go to a different school.

2 (have / new friends)
  _____

3 (Elaine / not be / my girlfriend)
  _____

4 (spend / all my free time on Skype)
  _____

What would have happened in the past if you had been really good at sport?

5 (I / win / lots of competitions)
  _____

6 (I / not do / so well in my exams last year)
  _____

7 (I / join / an athletics club)
  _____
  _____

8 (the local paper / interview me and / publish / my photo)
  _____

Grammar Alive Hypothesising

6 *** Make dialogues from the cues.**

A: Do you like dancing?

B: No, I don't. [1]If / like / dancing / I ask Debbie for a dance last Saturday
  If I liked dancing, I would have asked Debbie for a dance last Saturday.

A: [2]If you / ask her / she say / yes
  _____

B: Really? Do you think so?

A: Did you win the game?

B: No. [3]If I / win / match / be / happier now
  _____

A: [4]If / train harder / last month / you / win
  _____

B: [5]Yes, but / if / train harder / not have time to study.
  _____

  [6]If / not study / not pass my exams last week.
  _____

Listening

1 **2.2** **Listen to five people talking about motorbikes. Match the people (1-5) with the sentences (a-c).**

a He/She rides a motorbike. _1_

b He/She doesn't ride a motorbike but likes them. ___ ___

c He/She doesn't ride a motorbike and is quite negative about them. ___ ___

2 **2.2** **Listen again. Match the people (1-5) with the statements (a-f). There is one extra statement.**

a Bikers should be more careful. ___

b The law is wrong. ___

c My parents are really worried. _1_

d Motorbikes are more and more popular. ___

e Young people now are different. ___

f It's a family tradition. ___

3 **2.2** **Complete the phrases from the dialogue with one word. Then listen again to check.**

1 Hello, there. How's it __going__ ?

2 **A:** OK, thanks a _____ .
  B: No _____ .

3 **A:** Hi, can I ask you a question?
  B: Yes, fire _____ .

4 It's something for all generations of our family, you know what I _____ ?

5 **A:** Can I ask you why not?
  B: Yeah, _____ . You _____ , people who are seventeen, like me, are not responsible enough for such a dangerous machine.

6 My granddad had a bike in the 60s and he and his friends had a wild _____ .

7 **A:** Can I ask you one last question about motorbikes?
  B: Okay, go _____ .

8 **A:** That's great. Thanks.
  B: No probs. See _____ .

Speaking

1 **Complete the dialogue with the words below.**

about   better   cool   could   don't   idea
let's   means   see   ~~thought~~   way

A: What do you want to do tomorrow?

B: I [1] _thought_ maybe we [2] _____ go to the beach.

A: That's a nice [3] _____ but it [4] _____ we'd have to get up really early.

B: We could leave tonight. That [5] _____ we could sleep there and we wouldn't be so tired.

A: [6] _____ ! Why [7] _____ we invite Jake and Neil, too.

B: Okay, I'll [8] _____ if they want to come.

A: I think we'd [9] _____ look on the internet for somewhere to stay first.

B: How [10] _____ taking a tent.

A: Okay, [11] _____ do that.

2 **Complete the dialogue with the correct form of the verbs in brackets.**

A: Do you want to go to the cinema tonight?

B: I'd rather we [1] ___did___ (do) something a bit different this week.

A: There's a concert on tonight. It's a punk band. How about [2] _____ (go) to that?

B: That's fine by me but [3] _____ (we / better ask) Dana first. She isn't very keen on loud music.

A: What if you [4] _____ (tell) her that it was a concert but not a punk concert. She [5] _____ (come) then, wouldn't she?

B: Probably but I'd rather you [6] _____ (tell) her because she [7] _____ (be) upset when she finds out.

A: Okay, why not? I don't mind if she's angry with me.

B: I suggest we [8] _____ (get) there quite early. It might be difficult to get tickets. What [9] _____ (you think) ?

A: Okay. Let's [10] _____ (meet) at 6.30.

B: Great, that's fine by me.

28

GRAMMAR
it and *there*

1 * Match the beginnings (1-8) with the correct endings (a-h).

1 It is _b_

2 It isn't ___

3 There are ___

4 There aren't ___

5 There is a ___

6 There isn't ___

7 It has ___

8 It hasn't ___

a enough information available about the problems of having a pet.

b clear that dogs are very loyal.

c been said that dogs are a man's best friend.

d a lot of animals which don't make good pets.

e had any exercise for three days.

f enough checks on people who want to own pets.

g problem with homeless animals in our area.

h fair to keep big dogs in a small flat.

2 * Complete the dialogue with *it* or *there.*

A: What do you think of our town?

B: Well, ¹___It___ is very safe. ²_____ isn't much crime, is there?

A: That's true. So you like it here?

B: Well, ³_____'s okay but ⁴_____'s quite boring. I mean, ⁵_____ isn't much to do.

A: No, that's true. I like it, though. ⁶_____'s a very friendly town. Everyone knows each other.

B: Yes, so ⁷_____'s no privacy.

A: Don't be so negative. Think of the good things. ⁸_____ are a lot of green spaces and ⁹_____ isn't polluted at all.

B: Don't you think so? ¹⁰_____ is a lot of traffic and I hate the centre. ¹¹_____'s always crowded and noisy.

A: But ¹²_____'s a rich town. ¹³_____ are lots of good shops and ¹⁴_____ isn't any homelessness.

3 ** Complete the sentences with the phrases below.

> is it   it is   ~~it isn't~~   it isn't   there is
> there are   there isn't   there aren't

1 _It isn't_ a very good party.

2 _____ many people here.

3 _____ evidence that chimpanzees are very intelligent.

4 _____ true that a chimpanzee could pass this exam?

5 _____ the world's worst zoo.

6 _____ more animals at the local pet shop.

7 _____ much food in here.

8 _____ a very full fridge.

4 *** Make sentences from the cues beginning with *It* or *There.*

1 any / good clubs / here
   There aren't any good clubs here.

2 impossible / find / anything to do in the evening
   _____

3 several / street gangs / this area
   _____

4 clear / should be more things / teenagers / do
   _____

5 lovely park near our house
   _____

6 much / graffiti / your town?
   _____

7 one of / nicest towns I / been to
   _____

8 true / this / very safe town
   _____

Writing Workshop 7

1 **Read the story and answer the questions.**

1 Where was the play being put on?
In the school hall.

2 Who was organising it?
_____

3 How did the writer feel before the play?
_____

4 What play were they putting on?
_____

5 What happened to the writer at the start of the play?
_____

6 What did he realise when he got up?
_____

7 How did he look when the play ended?
_____

8 How did Mr Roberts look when the writer said he wanted to be in another play?
_____

---

¹W_hile_____ getting ready for the play, we could hear people entering the school hall. We heard laughter and then silence ²a_____ Mr Roberts, the English teacher who had organised the play, entered the hall. I looked at my friends getting changed and wishing each other luck. I said nothing.

³S_____ , a door opened and Mr Roberts put his head round the door. 'Are you all ready?' he said cheerfully. I felt sick but there was no escape. He ⁴t_____ left and we could hear him talking to the parents and students in the hall. 'Ladies and gentlemen,' he said, 'Park High Drama Club are proud to present _Romeo and Juliet._' I only had a small part in the play but my character was the first to speak. I strode out onto the stage but, ⁵u_____ , before I had a chance to speak, I fell over. The audience laughed loudly ⁶w_____ I was trying to stand up. Having got up, my mind went completely blank. My friend came onto the stage and ⁷i_____ started speaking until I was able to continue. ⁸A_____ t_____ , my nervousness slowly disappeared and, ⁹I_____ , I didn't make any more mistakes. The audience cheered and we left the stage to get changed back into our normal clothes.

¹⁰A_____ , Mr Roberts came to congratulate us and he asked if we wanted to be in the next play. The first person to put up their hand was me. I'm not sure if Mr Roberts was pleased or not but he did look surprised!

---

2 **Complete the text with one word in each gap (1–10).**

3 **Choose the correct answers.**

1 I got into the bath but, _b_ the phone rang.
  a luckily   **b** immediately   **c** after that

2 I made friends and ___ , life at the new school got better.
  a after   **b** after that   **c** after then

3 ___ eating my lunch, I found a spider in my lunch box.
  a While   **b** As   **c** Afterwards

4 I wrote an article for the school newsletter but, ___ , they didn't want to publish it.
  a afterwards   **b** luckily   **c** unfortunately

5 ___ we came off the football pitch at the end of the match, the crowd cheered loudly.
  a While   **b** As   **c** Then

6 We ___ decided to have a party to welcome the new students.
  a afterwards   **b** after that   **c** then

Sentence Builder Sequence linking

4 **Completes sentences a–c so that they have the same meaning as the first sentence.**

1 The teacher caught me using my mobile phone and sent me to the head teacher.
  a After _catching me using my mobile phone, the_ _teacher sent me to the head teacher._
  b Having _____
  c After he _____

2 I asked Jenny out and stood there shaking nervously.
  a Having _____
  b After I _____
  c After _____

5 **Read the instructions and write a story beginning with the words below. Use a real event or make one up.**

'One of the most important lessons I have learned in life was when I …'

- Set the scene and say how you were feeling.
- Say what happened and how you felt.
- Say how you felt afterwards and how other people reacted.
- Say how you feel about the experience now.

Write between 120 and 180 words.

Check Your Progress 7

❶ Communities Match the beginnings (1–8) with the correct endings (a–h).

1 You should lock ___
2 We all help each ___
3 It's safe for children to go ___
4 We should all vote ___
5 The council should let us all take part ___
6 The problem is that we have ___
7 I like people who keep ___
8 One thing this town lacks is ___

a in local elections.
b out on their own.
c your front door at night.
d to themselves.
e in decision-making.
f decent sanitation.
g no privacy.
h other out.

/8

❷ Multi-part verbs (3) Choose the correct answers.

1 Your birthday was three weeks ago. It's about time these balloons in the living room came ___ .
   a away   b over   c down
2 If you don't get ___ with your work now, you won't be able to go out at the weekend.
   a in   b off   c on
3 At last, everything was ready and we were ___ .
   a off   b up   c out
4 The others have headed ___ to the campsite.
   a through   b in   c on
5 Can you help me set ___ this tent?
   a out   b up   c off
6 I saw Tom and Nick hanging ___ near the playground.
   a around   b along   c away

/6

❸ Verb of perception + infinitive/-ing form Make sentences from the cues.

1 / you see / Paul / drive / his parents' car yesterday when you were shopping in town?
   _____

2 Yesterday / we listen / a Year Eight student / play the whole of Beethoven's 'Moonlight Sonata'.
   _____

3 I / catch / my little brother / try on / my leather jacket yesterday
   _____

4 Before I switched off the radio yesterday / hear / a politician / say / there was no crime in our area
   _____

/4

❹ Conditionals Complete the sentences with the correct form of the verbs in brackets.

1 If we _____ (know) our neighbours we would ask them round for a drink sometimes.
2 If I'd known there was a gang of burglars in our town, I _____ (not leave) the front door unlocked last weekend.
3 If I _____ (not see) this film last week, I'd go to see it with my friends this evening.
4 I _____ (not go) to the youth club so often if there was somewhere else to hang out.
5 If the library opened on Saturdays, I _____ (take) my books back last weekend.
6 I _____ (not have) any money now if I hadn't started working in a shop last year.
7 If you _____ (tell) me about the concert, I would have gone with you.
8 If there were more policemen on the streets, there _____ (not be) so much vandalism last week.

/8

❺ it and there Complete the dialogue with it or there in the gaps.

A: I went to the youth club yesterday. ¹_____ was great. ²_____ were loads of people there. You should come.
B: Yes, but ³_____ is a long way from my house and ⁴_____ aren't many buses in the evening.
B: ⁵_____'s okay, my dad can take you. ⁶_____'s room for one more in the car.
A: Oh right. Great. ⁷_____'s boring at home alone. ⁸_____'s not a lot to do if everyone else is out.

/4

TOTAL SCORE **/30**

Module Diary

❶ Look at the objectives on page 65 in the Students' Book. Choose three and evaluate your learning.

1 Now I can _____
   well / quite well / with problems.
2 Now I can _____
   well / quite well / with problems.
3 Now I can _____
   well / quite well / with problems.

❷ Look at your results. What language areas in this module do you need to study more?

Sound Choice 4

Sound Check

Say the words and expressions below.

a It does look nice. I did do it myself. He was definitely a genius. (Exercise 1)

b If I'd known the answers, I wouldn't've failed. (Exercise 2)

c solution, pollution, university, sanitation (Exercise 3)

d daughter, lot, now, boy (Exercise 4)

e church, this, photo (Exercise 5)

f What do you mean by that exactly? That's a good idea but it means we'd have to leave early in the morning. (Exercise 6)

g ambitious, sensible (Exercise 7)

h history, historic (Exercise 8)

2.3 **Listen and check your answers. Which sounds and expressions did you have problems with? Choose three exercises to do below.**

1 **2.4** Grammar - sentence stress **Listen to the sentences and underline the stressed word.**

1 It <u>does</u> look nice.
2 I <u>did</u> do it myself.
3 He was <u>definitely</u> a genius.
4 It can't be true.
5 He seems to be asleep.
6 You do look ill.
7 People tend to believe what they read.
8 You're bound to win.

2 **2.5** Grammar - contractions and weak forms in contractions **Listen to the sentences and repeat them.**

1 If I'd known the answers, I wouldn't've failed.
2 You'd've enjoyed the film if you'd come with us.
3 We'd've been on time if you hadn't forgotten your money.
4 If he'd told the truth, he wouldn't've got into so much trouble.
5 If I hadn't taken my camera, I wouldn't've been able to take any photos.

3 **2.6** Consonants - before vowels **Listen to the words and repeat them.**

1 solution
2 pollution
3 evolution
4 reclusive
5 volunteer
6 university
7 sanitation
8 anniversary
9 niece
10 uniform

4 **2.7** Vowels - /ɔː/, /ɒ/, /aʊ/, /ɔɪ/ **Listen to the four vowel sounds and the example. Then write the words you hear in the correct column.**

/ɔː/	/ɒ/	/aʊ/	/ɔɪ/
or	got	now	boy

5 **2.8** Spelling **Listen and complete the words with the first or last two letters.**

1 _ch_urch
2 __all
3 __is
4 __oto
5 __ere
6 __een
7 gra__
8 __iz
9 cra__
10 __ether
11 wor__
12 tou__

6 **2.9** Expressions **Listen to the sentences and repeat the underlined sections.**

1 <u>What do you mean by</u> that exactly?
2 <u>That's a good idea but</u> it means we'd have to leave early in the morning.
3 <u>In other words,</u> you need more money.
4 <u>So that means</u> there are four different teams taking part, right?
5 <u>Cool! That way we</u> share the work between us.
6 <u>That's fine by me but I'd rather</u> you didn't book the tickets until I've asked my parents.
7 <u>Okay, I'll see if</u> he wants to come.
8 <u>As I said before,</u> there are a few more things to do.

7 **2.10** Difficult words **Repeat the schwa sound /ə/ and then underline the part(s) of each word with this sound.**

1 metic<u>ul</u>ous
2 ambitious
3 self-confident
4 clever
5 fearless
6 driven
7 logical
8 sensible
9 computer
10 serious

8 **2.11** Difficult words - shifting word stress **Look at the pairs of words. Underline the stressed syllable. Then listen to check.**

1 <u>or</u>ganise   organi<u>sa</u>tion
2 economy   economic
3 personal   personality
4 history   historic
5 enthusiasm   enthusiastic
6 environment   environmental

LANDMARKS

TOPIC TALK – VOCABULARY

1 Label the pictures.

1 d_esert_

5 g_____

2 f_____

6 b_____

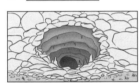

3 c_____

7 s_____

4 g_____

8 c_____

2 Complete the sentences with the words below.

coniferous deciduous farmland hills
prairie ~~sandy~~ shingle valleys

This end of the beach is nice to sit on because it's ¹_____sandy_____ . The other end is mainly ²_____ so it's a bit uncomfortable.

We walked over the mountains to our new home. When we arrived, it was all ³_____ with long grass but we planted some crops and turned it into ⁴_____ so we could grow enough food to eat and sell.

There are quite high ⁵_____ all around but most people live in the river ⁶_____ where there is water and not so much snow.

It's beautiful here in the autumn because our forests are mainly ⁷_____ so the leaves change colour to yellow, orange and gold. In the winter, there aren't any leaves because there are no ⁸_____ forests.

3 Match the definitions (1-10) with the words (a-j).

1 A tower which guides ships away from danger at night. _e_

2 A very tall modern building. ___

3 It carries water across a river or valley. ___

4 A large, strong building built in the past as a defence against attack. ___

5 The main church of an area. ___

6 A round roof on a building. ___

7 A tall solid stone post used to support a building or as a decoration. ___

8 An image of a person or animal made from a material such as stone or metal. ___

9 A structure with a curved top and straight sides which supports the weight of a bridge or building. ___

10 It allows people to cross a river, road or valley. ___

a bridge
b cathedral
c dome
d aqueduct
e lighthouse
f column
g castle
h arch
i skyscraper
j statue

4 Complete the text with one letter in each gap.

The ¹l _a_ n d _s c a_ p _e_ here consists of farmland, low ²h _ l _ s and river valleys. Where I live, there are also some shingle ³b _ _ c _ _ _ with cliffs behind them. There are some interesting ⁴c _ _ _ s in the cliffs but it can be dangerous to go into them because rocks often fall from their roofs.

The ⁵a _ _ _ a I like best is some ⁶m _ _ r _ _ n _ near here. It is very beautiful and quiet. It's a good place to walk but you have to stay on the paths because there are dangerous ⁷m _ _ s _ _ s and you can sink down into the mud if you aren't careful. My favourite ⁸n _ _ u _ _ l landmark is a waterfall 2 km from my house. It is a very popular place for picnics.

There are some interesting ⁹m _ _ -m _ _ _ landmarks near my town. There is a beautiful ¹⁰p _ l _ _ _ where a prince and princess once lived. There is also a very famous cathedral with unusual ¹¹s _ _ _ n _ _ glass windows.

29 GRAMMAR
Relative clauses

REMEMBER

Complete Exercises A-B before you start this lesson.

A Complete the sentences with the correct relative pronoun. Sometimes two may be possible.

1 This castle was built by a king _who/that_ ruled this area 800 years ago.
2 There is a stone circle here _____ experts believe is over 4000 years old.
3 The bridge _____ crosses the river here was closed for six months because of floods.
4 That's the office block _____ my dad works.
5 In 2009, _____ we went on holiday to Cornwall, we stayed in an old lighthouse.
6 My friend, _____ house is next to a lake, goes sailing every day in the summer.
7 The landscape is _____ I like best about my country.
8 Paula Keller, _____ makes statues from marble, is having an exhibition here next week.

B Combine the sentences to make one sentence using the relative pronoun in brackets.

1 There is a forest near my home. It is very big. (which)
   There is a forest near my home which is very big.
2 I remember the day. We first met on that day. (when)
   _____
   _____
3 This is the beach. We used to come here every summer. (where)
   _____
   _____
4 We learned about a king and queen at school. They are buried in the tombs under our local church. (who)
   _____
   _____
5 I loved the old buildings in our town. They were knocked down recently. (that)
   _____
   _____
6 I read about Charlie Chaplin. His statue is in our town centre. (whose)
   _____
   _____

❶ * Complete the sentences with the relative clauses below.

when we arrived   which starts in Catania
which are to the north of Sicily
~~which is Italy's highest volcano~~   where we stayed
who took us to the airport   who was a Roman poet
whose son we looked after one evening

1 Mount Etna, _which is Italy's highest volcano_ , is in Sicily.
2 Virgil, _____ , wrote about an eruption in *The Aeneid*.
3 You can get great views of Mount Etna from the Circumetnea train, _____ .
4 There are also volcanoes on the Aeolian Islands, _____ .
5 The hotel in Taormina _____ had great views of Mount Etna.
6 The day _____ was cloudy and we couldn't see anything.
7 The family _____ gave us some maps of the local area.
8 The taxi driver _____ drove really fast.

❷ ** Complete the sentences with the relative pronoun in capitals in the correct places. Add commas where necessary.

1 (WHO) My dad‚ who helped us put up the tent‚ was worried it would rain.
2 (WHICH) Pompeii was destroyed by a volcanic eruption is one of Italy's most popular tourist attractions.
3 (WHERE) The place we spent most of our holiday was the sandy beach in front of our hotel.
4 (WHO) I was grateful to the people looked after us when we lost our money.
5 (WHERE) Lanzarote we went on holiday last year has got black sand because of lava.
6 (THAT) The villages were destroyed by the volcanic eruption have been rebuilt.
7 (WHOSE) Mr Jenkins plane was delayed by a volcanic eruption came back to school one week late.
8 (WHO) We thanked Mr Simpson helped us when our bags were stolen.
9 (WHOSE) The people homes were destroyed received money and help from the government.
10 (WHO) The man met us was very friendly.

❸ ** **Complete the second sentences so that they end with a preposition.**

1 The Decade Volcanoes are the sixteen volcanoes about which experts are most worried.
The Decade Volcanoes are the sixteen volcanoes
_____*which experts are most worried about.*_____

2 The EU is one organisation from which the Decade Volcano Project gets money.
The EU is one organisation _____
_____

3 The project helped to save the town of Zafferana in 1992 towards which lava was flowing.
The project helped to save the town of Zafferana in 1992 _____
_____

4 There was an eruption at a volcano in Columbia inside which scientists were exploring.
There was an eruption at a volcano in Columbia
_____

5 The eruption was a sudden one from which they were unable to escape.
The eruption was a sudden one _____
_____

❹ *** **Match the sentences (1–6) with the sentences (a–f) which naturally follow them. Then make one sentence using a sentential relative clause.**

1 In 1792, there was an eruption from Mount Unzen. _*b*_

2 In 1989, there were several earthquakes near Mount Unzen. ___

3 Many people lived near to the volcano. ___

4 There were several eruptions between 1991 and 1994. ___

5 In 1999, scientists started drilling inside the volcano. ___

6 The temperature inside the volcano was 155°C. ___

a It meant that they were in danger from the lava.

b It caused a mega tsunami.

c They hoped that this would help them to understand volcanoes better.

d These eruptions destroyed over 2000 homes.

e This was much lower than the 500°C scientists had expected.

f They caused another eruption.

1 _*In 1792, there was a volcanic eruption from Mount*_
   *Unzen, which caused a mega tsunami.*

2 _____

3 _____

4 _____

5 _____

6 _____

Grammar Alive Adding comments

❺ *** **Make sentences from the cues using *which*, *whose* or *where*.**

1 The Nile / longest river in / world / flow / through ten countries
   *The Nile, which is the longest river in the world,*
   *flows through ten countries.*

2 The Kröller-Müller museum / you can see many paintings by van Gogh / in the Netherlands.
   _____

3 The Logan Rock / weighs 80 tons / move / slightly when it / pushed
   _____

4 Nea Filadelfia / in the north of Athens / often have / 30 mm more rain in January / the south of Athens
   _____

5 Malibu Beach / many film stars live / have / 34 km of coast
   _____

6 The city of Bath / Roman baths can still be used / be / in west of England
   _____

7 Colima / erupted more than forty times since 1576 / be / one of / most active volcanoes / North America
   _____

8 St Paul's Cathedral / dome / one of / biggest in / world / designed by Sir Christopher Wren
   _____

❻ *** **Complete the dialogue using the cues and *which*, *who* or *where*.**

A: Where did you go on holiday last year?

B: [1](Venice – really beautiful) I went
   _____*to Venice, which was really beautiful.*_____

A: Who did you go with?

B: [2](two friends – been there before) I went
   _____

A: Where did you stay?

B: [3](old palace – near St Mark's Square) We stayed
   _____

A: What did you do?

B: [4](gondola ride – I loved) We went
   _____

   [5](great gondolier – really funny) We had
   _____

A: Where did you eat?

B: [6](restaurant in our hotel – ate there every night)
   There was _____

1 **Read the text. Match the sentences (a-h) with the gaps (1-7). There is one extra sentence.**

a They then take a fifty-minute boat ride to the island itself.

b However, not everywhere on the island is so destroyed.

c That's why they decided to build a small city there.

d For those brave enough to go inside, there are even more interesting sights.

e However, surprisingly, tunnels which were built under the city can still be used safely.

f They do worry, though, about being caught on the island.

g It was the most crowded city in the world.

h A small part of the island was opened to tourists in 2009.

Hashima Island is one of many small islands off the coast of Japan not far from the city of Nagasaki. In the late nineteenth century, coal was found under the island and it was bought by the Mitsubishi company. It wasn't easy to bring the workers to the island by boat every day. ¹ _c_ Because of the island's very small size, the company built concrete apartment blocks. At one stage the population was over five thousand. ² ___ Then, in January 1974, Mitsubishi announced that it was closing the mines. By April, everyone had left.

Despite the solidity of the buildings and the thickness of their walls, many have collapsed or started to show signs of deterioration in the forty years since the people left. Windows are broken and the lack of maintenance means that it is too dangerous for anyone to enter the buildings. ³ ___

Hashima Island, though, has recently seen the return of some people. ⁴ ___ Unfortunately, it would cost too much to make the rest of the island safe. The reason for the interest in the island, apart from its unusual history, is seeing how the world would look if humans were to suddenly disappear. The only legal way to visit the island is on a guided tour from Nagasaki. There are two departures every day except on Tuesdays. Before leaving for the island, tourists visit a museum about its history. ⁵ ___ There, they can stand on three specially built platforms from which they can look at the ruins.

However, although private visits to the island are illegal, some people have managed to get there. First of all they need to find a fisherman willing to take them. They must set off very early in the morning and hope that the weather allows them to land. Once there, most of these illegal visitors spend their time taking photos. The ruined apartment blocks and the plants growing in and around them make interesting subjects to photograph. ⁶ ___ Most of the flats were left empty but there are one or two signs of humanity. A wooden toy, broken hospital equipment, and other objects lie unwanted on the dusty, destroyed floors.

Soon, though, it is time to leave. Most photographers are unworried by the danger of falling concrete. ⁷ ___ That's why they have to leave before the first tourist boat arrives. What would happen if they were to be found on the island? According to Japanese law, they could be sent to prison for thirty days. That's why finding a fisherman willing to take you there isn't always easy.

2 Read the text and decide whether the statements are true (T), false (F) or if there is no information to decide (NI).

1 No one knows why people decided to live on the island. _F_

2 The workers weren't allowed to stay on the island after the mines closed down. ___

3 The buildings weren't very well-made. ___

4 The tunnels under the city haven't been destroyed. ___

5 The reason why the whole island hasn't been opened for visitors is the cost. ___

6 The museum is on the island. ___

7 The weather in the area is often bad. ___

8 There is nothing left in any of the apartments. ___

9 People going to the island with fishermen often return on tourist boats. ___

Word Builder Noun endings

3 Complete the text with the correct form of the words in capitals.

The ¹ _population_ of Centralia in Pennsylvania, USA, in 1962 was 3000. The ² _____ of the town was due to the coal under the ground it was built on but this is also what destroyed it. The coal was accidentally set alight in 1962 when residents were burning rubbish. Nothing could stop the fires. The people tried for twenty years but finally, in 1982, when the fires threatened their ³ _____ , the government gave them money to move to new homes. The ⁴ _____ of almost every person left Centralia a ghost town. The main road was moved away from the town and the fires still burned. However, despite the ⁵ _____ of almost all signs of civilisation, and the ⁶ _____ of the buildings, about twenty people stayed on, living in those homes that hadn't been destroyed.	POPULATE GROW SURVIVE DEPART DISAPPEAR DETERIORATE
By 2010, this number had fallen to ten. The ⁷ _____ of the houses in the town, and their ⁸ _____ to fire, led to the authorities to make it illegal for anyone to stay there.	VULNERABLE EXPOSE
It's not clear if there are still any residents fighting to stay on.	

Sentence Builder Conditionals

4 Rewrite the sentences with the correct form of the verb in brackets.

1 What would happen if this volcano erupted? (ERUPT)
   What would happen if this volcano were to erupt?

2 What would happen to us if these walls collapsed? (COLLAPSE)

   _____

3 What would we do if everyone left this town? (LEAVE)

   _____

4 What would your parents say if you joined a rock band? (JOIN)

   _____

   _____

5 What would you do if your brother destroyed your computer? (DESTROY)

   _____

   _____

6 What would you think if someone offered you a free holiday to Australia? (OFFER)

   _____

   _____

7 What would your teacher say if the whole class failed their exams? (FAIL)

   _____

   _____

Listening

1 **2.12** Listen to a tour guide telling people about the Forth Bridge in Scotland. Match the numbers with what they relate to (a–g).

8 _b_   2528 ___   3.2 million ___
4600 ___   46 ___   130 million ___
57 ___

a The number of people who died building the bridge.
b The number of years it took to build the bridge.
c The cost of painting the bridge in pounds.
d The height of the railway above the river in metres.
e The length of the bridge in metres.
f The cost of building the bridge in pounds.
g The number of people who worked on the bridge.

2 **2.12** Listen again. Decide whether the sentences are true (T), false (F) or if there is no information (NI).

1 The first bridge across the Firth of Forth was a railway bridge. _T_
2 The fifty-seven people who died all drowned. ___
3 If the bridge was built today, it would cost about £235 million. ___
4 The Tay Bridge disaster happened before the Forth Bridge was built. ___
5 The designer of the Forth Bridge was the same man who designed the Tay Bridge. ___
6 'Painting the Forth Bridge' is a saying which is only used in Scotland. ___
7 The reason why it isn't painted so often now is that it costs too much. ___
8 The old paint had never been cleaned off before the most recent repainting of the bridge. ___

Sentence Builder Expressions + -ing forms or infinitives

3 Complete the sentences using the cues in brackets.

1 _There's no point trying_ (There/point/try) to get a ticket on the day of a performance because they sell out very quickly.
2 _____ (It/worth/get) here when the sun is going down.
3 If you stand here on a windy day, _____ (it/important/hold) on to your hat.
4 _____ (it/worth/eat) because it's very cheap.
5 _____ (it/good/leave) most of your money locked in your hotel room when you go out sightseeing.
6 _____ (There/point/wait) for a bus today. There aren't any on Sundays.
7 _____ (It/good/check) on the internet to find the best places to visit.
8 _____ (It/important/take) a map when you walk in the forest.

Speaking

1 **2.13** Complete the sentences using the cues. Then listen to check your answers.

1 A: What do you think I should take?
   B: _I'd recommend taking_ (recommend / take) a warm coat.
   C: _____ (advise / take) a good guidebook.
   D: _____ (suggest / take) a camera.
2 A: I've never been to Rome before.
   B: _____ (better / take) a map.
   C: _____ (I / advise / learn) some Italian.
   D: _____ (If / I / you / I / go) on an organised tour.
3 A: I don't know where to eat.
   B: _____ (I / not recommend / eat) at one of the tourist restaurants in the town centre.
   C: _____ (worth / look) for restaurant reviews on the internet.
   D: _____ (there / point / eat) fast food. You can eat that at home.

LESSON **32** GRAMMAR

Emphasis: nominal relatives

1 * **Rewrite the sentences using the relative pronoun *what*.**

1 The thing I remember most about Rome is the Coliseum.
What I remember most about Rome is the Coliseum.

2 The thing I disliked about Rome was the traffic.
_____
_____

3 The thing that annoyed me about Paris was queuing for everything.
_____
_____

4 The thing I couldn't believe about Cairo was the driving.
_____
_____

5 When I arrived in Athens, the thing I most wanted to do was to visit the Acropolis.
_____
_____

6 The thing that made me want to stay in Barcelona was the nightlife.
_____

7 The thing that surprised me about Amsterdam was how small it was.
_____
_____

8 The thing that I didn't realise about Warsaw was that it had been completely destroyed in the war.
_____
_____

2 * **Replace the words in brackets with *what* or *whatever*.**

1 Tell them _____*what*_____ (the things) you found out from your guidebook.

2 You can buy _____ (anything) you want here.

3 I'll get you _____ (everything) you need.

4 I don't know _____ (the right words) to say.

5 Do you remember _____ (the events that) happened last night?

6 _____ (Everything) I do makes Emma angry.

7 This book tells you _____ (the things that) you can do in the evening.

8 You pay €10 and then you can eat _____ (anything and as much as) you want.

3 ** **Put the words in brackets in the correct order.**

1 (liked / the hotel / What / was / most / I / about)
_____*What I liked most about the hotel*_____ was the bathroom.

2 (I / was / didn't / What / know)
_____ that this hotel used to be a palace.

3 (What / do / wanted / we / to / was)
_____ to go on a boat trip.

4 (meant / was / was / I / that / What / the hotel)
_____ nice but overpriced.

5 (is / we / usually / What / do)
_____ book a last-minute holiday.

6 (they / do / is / What / should)
_____ paint the buildings in the town centre.

4 *** **Complete the second sentence so that it has the same meaning as the first.**

1 The new art gallery in the town was really amazing.
What *was really amazing was the new art gallery in the town.*

2 We really need a good guidebook.
What _____

3 The weather was disappointing.
What _____

4 The amazing thing about the place was how quiet it was.
What _____
_____

5 We realised that we were in the wrong queue.
What _____
_____

6 The Thai restaurant in this market is excellent.
What _____
_____

7 We decided to take a taxi back to the hotel.
What _____
_____

8 You must go and see the beautiful old church on the hill.
What _____
_____

9 We want to do a Spanish course in Madrid.
What _____
_____

10 We liked the people who worked in the hotel.
What _____
_____

Writing Workshop 8

1 Read the text and match the headings (A-E) to the paragraphs (1-4). There is one extra heading.

A Things to do in St Ives
B The writer's opinion of St Ives
C Memories of St Ives
D Where St Ives is
E The history of St Ives

ST IVES

1 _C_
SURFING in the clear water, looking at the eye-catching paintings in the Tate Gallery, relaxing with a tasty ice cream on the beach, meeting cool, friendly people. This is what I think of when I remember the beautiful town of St Ives.

2 ___
St Ives in Cornwall is in an extraordinary location with picturesque beaches all round the town centre. Some face north and have great waves for surfing. Others which face south are protected from the wind and are perfect for small children. The views from the hills and cliffs around St Ives are breathtaking and, when it is too cold for swimming, it is a perfect place for walking.

3 ___
You will never be bored in St Ives. In the morning, you can go shopping along the main street with its fascinating craft and souvenir shops. In the afternoon, why not take a boat trip to Seal Island to see these fascinating animals in their natural surroundings. There is delicious food available for all tastes and budgets from filling snacks to expensive, high-class restaurants. The nightlife isn't as wild as in nearby Newquay, but it's still fun.

4 ___
Of course, St Ives does have its problems. It gets uncomfortably crowded in the summer and the town centre streets become filled with traffic as people search for one of the limited parking spaces available. The seagulls are also a problem as they have got used to people and have been known to steal food from people's hands as they picnic on the beach. However, for me, it is a wonderful place to spend the summer and the locals are always warm and hospitable. I'm going again this summer.

2 Read the description again and complete the table below with words from the text.

Attractive to look at	Very good / interesting	Friendly and pleasant
1 e _ye-catching_	5 e_____	11 w_____
2 be_____	6 g_____	12 h_____
3 p_____	7 p_____	
4 br_____	8 f_____	
	9 d_____	
	10 w_____	

3 Choose the correct words.

1 The _picturesque_/delicious castle is worth visiting.
2 The people are very hospitable/breathtaking.
3 The view from our hotel room was sociable/spectacular.
4 The new tower is quite welcoming/striking.
5 The waiters were very marvellous/welcoming.
6 The new airport is very impressive/good-natured.

4 Look at the information about New York City and put the words and phrases under the correct heading.

the Statue of Liberty, can be dangerous after dark, go shopping on 5th Avenue, ~~riding on the subway~~, eating hot dogs, see a play on Broadway, incredibly crowded at rush hour, the Empire State Building, take a boat trip around Manhattan, seeing Central Park, Tiffany's Department Store, fascinating and amazing city, looking up at the skyscrapers, sociable and hospitable people, the Brooklyn Bridge, go to the top of the Empire State Building and look at the view

Memories	Landmarks
riding on the subway	_____
_____	_____
_____	_____
_____	_____
_____	_____
Things to do	**Opinions**
_____	_____
_____	_____
_____	_____
_____	_____

5 Imagine you have just come back from a trip to New York City. Read the instructions and use the ideas in Exercise 4 or your own ideas to write a description of the city.

• Introduce the text with some memories.
• Describe the landmarks.
• Talk about what you can do there.
• Give your opinions about the city.

Write between 180 and 250 words.

Check Your Progress 8

① Landmarks Complete the words with one letter in each gap.

Landscape features
1 g _ _ c _ _ r _
2 e _ _ u _ r _ _ s

Man-made landmarks
3 c _ _ r _ h
4 a _ _ _ d _ c _

Materials
5 c _ _ c _ _ t _
6 m _ _ b _ _

Architectural features
7 c _ l _ _ n _
8 g _ _ s _ p _ n _ _ s

/8

② Relative clauses Combine the sentences using the word in capitals.

1 Mark is a good player. We depend on him. (WHO)
Mark _____ on.

2 There was a problem with the heating at school. It meant that we had to go home. (WHICH) There _____ home.

3 This is the school hall. We do our exams in here. (WHERE) This _____ exams.

4 Tom is a great writer. I read his blog every day. (WHOSE) Tom _____ day.

5 The sports day took place last week. I was in bed, ill. (WHEN) Last _____ , ill.

6 This is my secret box. I keep my diary in here. (WHICH) This _____ diary.

/6

③ Noun endings Complete the sentences with the correct form of the words below.

arrive   depart   disappear   maintain
populate   survive   weak

1 What's the _____ of Germany?
2 My main _____ is that I can't concentrate.
3 The security guards were shocked by the sudden _____ of the painting.
4 Our _____ depends on us finding a way to create clean energy.
5 My friend's party came to a sudden end with the unexpected _____ of his parents.
6 We were sitting on the plane when we heard that our _____ had been delayed for four hours.
7 They were doing important _____ work on the roads, which made our journey very slow.

/7

④ Conditionals Complete the conditionals with the correct form of the verbs in brackets.

1 What _____ (you do) if your phone _____ (be) to disappear suddenly?

2 If the rain _____ (be) to stop, this land _____ (become) desert.

3 If we were _____ (find) a map showing you where there was a ruined city, _____ (you look) for it?

4 If someone was _____ (tell) you that there was a ghost in this castle, _____ (you stay) here for the night?

/4

⑤ Emphasis: nominal relatives Rewrite the sentences starting with _What_.

1 We want to go swimming.
_____
_____

2 I didn't know that it was someone else's seat.
_____
_____

3 I can't tell you the name of the hotel.
_____
_____

4 I don't like big cities.
_____
_____

5 My parents told me to be careful.
_____
_____

/5

TOTAL SCORE   /30

Module Diary

① Look at the objectives on page 75 in the Students' Book. Choose three and evaluate your learning.

1 Now I can _____
well / quite well / with problems.

2 Now I can _____
well / quite well / with problems.

3 Now I can _____
well / quite well / with problems.

② Look at your results. What language areas in this module do you need to study more?

Exam Choice 4

Reading

1 Read the text. Decide whether the sentences are true (T), false (F) or if there is no information (NI).

1 The writer would like to meet everyone else in her community. ___

2 She has been hostelling all over the world. ___

3 One good thing about hostelling is that it is cheap. ___

4 She prefers to have a single room when travelling. ___

5 Her holiday last year was the first time she had stayed in hostels. ___

6 She couldn't have stayed in a cheaper room at the hostel. ___

7 The girl was upset about the noise in the hostel. ___

8 The girl travelled with the girls from Denmark after they left Prague. ___

Happy hostelling!

I belong to a community. There are thousands of us all over the world. I'll never meet all of them, I don't even think I'd want to, but they are all my friends. In fact, our motto is that 'a stranger is a friend I haven't met yet'. We are the hostelling community and our members stay in hostels everywhere.

The great thing about hostelling, apart from the low prices of course, is that you meet so many different kinds of people. The bedrooms usually have between four and ten beds in them. I can't imagine staying in a normal hotel and locking myself into a room all alone. How boring that would be! At a hostel, there is always someone there to welcome you and give you advice about places to see and where to go to eat. Actually, I prefer to eat in the hostels themselves if I can because the food is generally tasty and cheap. In most hostels now, there are proper canteens with people employed to work there. I prefer the smaller hostels where the guests are supposed to help with preparing the meals or cleaning up after them.

Last year I went on a tour of Europe and stayed in hostels everywhere. I had a great time. My favourite place was Prague. I didn't stay at an official youth hostel – I'm not even sure if there is one – but I found a great private one. I stayed in a room for twelve people. That was the cheapest they had. £10 – what a bargain! It was a bit noisy at night but I think I was the one who made the most noise! The people working there were all friendly and helpful and the hostel was close to most of the famous landmarks like the old clock and the Charles Bridge. The bar was cool and the hostel was open 24 hours a day so I didn't have to hurry back in the evening. I liked Prague because the streets felt safe, even after dark and there were some good restaurants. Jan, a boy who worked in reception told us which areas of the city not to go to. He was from Prague and he knew everything! He helped us get cheap passes for the trams and underground and he even took one girl to hospital when she sprained her ankle on the stairs one night.

I met some cool girls from Denmark and we spent most of our time together. Unfortunately, when it was time to leave, I headed east to Hungary and they went north to Germany. I've kept in touch with them, though, and we're going to meet up next summer. I can't wait!

2 Read the text again and choose the correct answers.

1 The writer:
   a knows all the other members of the community.
   b has met all the other members of the community.
   c considers all the other members of the community to be her friends.
   d doesn't like everyone who is a member of the community.

2 When you go hostelling you:
   a sometimes have to do some work in the hostel.
   b aren't told anything about the town you are in.
   c have to go somewhere else to eat.
   d always know the people you are sharing a room with.

3 One thing she <u>doesn't</u> mention as an advantage about the hostel in Prague was:
   a the price.
   b the location.
   c the food.
   d the staff.

4 Jan helped the writer:
   a get to hospital.
   b get to know two Danish girls.
   c find her way round the city on the public transport.
   d avoid dangerous areas of the city.

Listening

3 **2.14** Listen to five people talking about places they have visited and match the speakers (1-5) with the sentences (a-f). There is one extra sentence.

   a The views were spectacular. ___
   b There was an impressive landmark. ___
   c It was too crowded. ___
   d The people were very welcoming. ___
   e The streets felt very safe. ___
   f There's a lot to do there. ___

4 **2.14** Listen again and decide whether the sentences are true (T), false (F) or if there is no information (NI).

1 The boy didn't go to the restaurant at the New Bridge. ___
2 The girl spoke French to the people from Colmar. ___
3 The girl didn't want to leave Arundel after her holiday. ___
4 The girl knew that she was going to Rome at a busy time of year. ___
5 The bridge across the gorge was crowded. ___

Speaking

5 Complete the dialogue with one word in each gap.

advise   don't   let's   means   not
point   rather   recommend   worth   you

Boy 1: Excuse me. Can you ¹_____ a good place to stay in Brighton that isn't too expensive?

Guide: I suggest ²_____ stay at the youth hostel. It's only £20 a night or you can have a room for three people for £50.

Boy 1: There are only two of us.

Boy 2: Why ³_____ we invite Steve? Then we could get the room cheaper.

Boy 1: Okay, why ⁴_____ ?

Guide: I'd ⁵_____ you to reserve a room very quickly. They are often full.

Boy 2: Okay, ⁶_____ do that now.

Boy 1: I'd ⁷_____ we waited. It ⁸_____ that, if Steve can't go, we'll have to pay £50 ourselves.

Boy 2: It's ⁹_____ risking it. I'm sure Steve will come. There's no ¹⁰_____ waiting.

Boy 1: Well, okay, if you think it's a good idea.

Exam Choice 4

Use of English

6 Complete the text with one word in each gap.

If my parents were [1]_____ move to a different town, I'd like them to move to Chichester in the south of England. [2]_____ is an old town but [3]_____ are lots of things for teenagers to do. I went there last year and [4]_____ I really liked about it were the shops and nightclubs. Luckily, I met two local teenagers [5]_____ took me to some cool places. If I hadn't met them, I'd [6]_____ been quite bored with just my parents for company. It's fine in the day but, in the evening I don't really want to sit in our hotel [7]_____ television, playing chess or reading!

I always try to do lots of sightseeing [8]_____ I go away. There's really [9]_____ point going somewhere and not getting to know the place, is there? Guidebooks are fine during the day. We visited lots of interesting places. There's an old cathedral in Chichester but my favourite place was in nearby Portsmouth [10]_____ we climbed a cool tower, [11]_____ has got a glass floor. It's quite scary looking down but the view from the top is spectacular. I just couldn't help thinking ... what if the glass in the floor [12]_____ to break?

Writing

7 Choose the correct answers.

1 ___ sitting in the back of the car, I could see the crowds of people looking at the stone circle.
   a While   **b** As   **c** After

2 ___ we got out of the car, we noticed the queues for tickets.
   a Afterwards   **b** While   **c** As

3 ___ , a man came and asked us if we were with a tour group.
   a Luckily   **b** After   **c** Unfortunately

4 He ___ told us we didn't have to queue as we weren't with a tour group.
   a after   **b** then   **c** afterwards

5 We ___ ran to the ticket office to get there before anyone else.
   a suddenly   **b** after that   **c** immediately

6 ___ , just at that moment, I fell over in some mud.
   a Luckily   **b** Immediately   **c** Unfortunately

7 I stood up and tried to clean my hands and trousers ___ my parents bought the tickets.
   a then   **b** while   **c** after

8 ___ that, we went to see the stone circle itself.
   a After   **b** Afterwards   **c** Then

9 We were walking round when ___ a rabbit ran out from the circle past all the tourists.
   a immediately   **b** as   **c** suddenly

10 We left the stones about an hour later. ___ , we went to the gift shop to buy some souvenirs.
   a Afterwards   **b** After   **c** While

8 Read the instructions and write a story about a visit to a famous place.

- Mention the situation – where you were and how you were feeling.
- Say what happened and how you felt.
- Say what happened later.
- Talk about how you feel about the visit now.

Write between 120 and 180 words.

TOPIC TALK – VOCABULARY

1 Read the clues and complete the names of the businesses.

1 You go to them to borrow or save money.
b_anks_____

2 You can drink coffee in them.
c_____

3 They are places which shows films.
c_____

4 They make things you can wear.
clothes m_____

5 You need them to be able to contact your friends.
mobile phone n_____
p_____

6 They take stories from authors and turn them into books.
p_____

7 Shops which can be found in lots of different towns.
c_____ s_____

8 You need them to travel by rail.
t_____ c_____

2 Complete the words with one letter in each gap.

Good services can be:
1 inexpensive.
2 e _ _ _ c _ _ _ t.
3 p _ _ c _ _ _ l.
4 r _ l _ _ b _ _ .

Good products are often:
5 good v _ _ _ e for m _ n _ _ .
6 good q _ _ l _ _ _ .
7 a _ _ r _ _ t _ _ _ .
8 h _ -t _ _ _ .

Bad services are often:
9 i _ _ f _ _ c _ _ _ _ .
10 u _ _ e _ _ a _ l _ .
11 u _ _ _ n _ _ u _ _ .

Bad products are sometimes:
12 o _ _ r-p _ _ c _ _ .
13 p _ _ r q _ _ l _ _ y.
14 u _ s _ _ e .

3 Replace the underlined phrases with one of the phrases below.

a family business   a multinational company   get a part-time job
get summer work   be self-employed   set up my own company
voluntary work   get work experience

1 I'm going to work for myself.   _be self-employed_

2 I'm going to work for a company which operates in many different countries. _____

3 I'm going to work in July and September.
_____

4 I'm going to work for a few hours each week.
_____

5 I'm going to do some work without pay. _____

6 I'm going to work with a company to learn more about the job and industry. _____

7 I'm going to start my own business. _____

8 I'm going to work for a company run by a husband and wife and their daughter. _____

4 Complete the dialogues with the words below.

ambition   assistant   experience   job   money
multinationals   opportunities   poor   priced   quality
reliable   services   shops   work

A: Can you tell me which kind of companies you prefer to buy goods and services from?

B: Well, with businesses such as corner [1]___shops___ , cafés and clubs, I prefer small companies. They are more friendly and their products and [2]_____ are usually more [3]_____ and better [4]_____ than large companies like [5]_____ can offer. I know that supermarkets and chain stores can sometimes offer products which are good value for [6]_____ but I often find that their products are [7]_____ quality. They might seem cheap but they are really over-[8]_____ .

A: Do you work at the moment?

B: Yes, I've got a part-time [9]_____ . I work on Saturdays as a shop [10]_____ . I've also done some voluntary [11]_____ in a shelter for homeless animals.

A: What would you like to do in the future?

B: My [12]_____ is to be a fashion designer but there are very few [13]_____ to get training. I'll probably do some unpaid work [14]_____ and hope that I get noticed and offered a job afterwards.

1 Make questions from the cues and then find the answers in the text.

1 What / Emil / do / when / thirteen?

What did Emil do when he was thirteen?

He borrowed money to buy a lawn mower.

2 How long / take / pay back / loan?

_____

_____

3 How / people / now employ / by his company?

_____

_____

4 How / sleep / he get / every night?

_____

_____

5 When / Juliette / have her idea?

_____

_____

6 What / her website / called?

_____

_____

7 What / she / do / when / sixteen?

_____

_____

8 Who / her website / for?

_____

_____

Teenage
SUCCESS
stories

Emil Motycka

Juliette Brindak

When Emil Motycka was thirteen, he borrowed money to buy a lawn mower. No one else in his area was offering a grass-cutting service so the door was open for him to earn some extra pocket money. It took him two years to pay back the loan and, since then he has proved to be an amazing businessman. He then became a student at the University of Colorado's Business School where he could probably have taught his lecturers something about running a business. Motycka Enterprises employs about sixty-five people and is growing all the time. The company doesn't just offer a grass-cutting service now. The workers can do almost anything from clearing snow to fixing Christmas lights and general building work.

Emil claims that his success is due to hard work and determination. That's why he only sleeps four hours a night! He rarely goes out because he feels that time spent not working and building up his business is time wasted.

It hasn't always been easy for Emil, especially in the early days when he was cutting lawns while his friends were going swimming or hanging out at the mall. However, his hard work soon paid off and he was the one who could buy a car and afford to take girlfriends somewhere better than the local burger bar.

Emil thinks that anyone can be a success if they work hard. As he says: 'The biggest failure you can have in life is not trying at all.'

Juliette Brindak's success story started when she was just ten years old. That's when she had the idea for the website Miss O and Friends. News of the website travelled quickly by word of mouth and she made her money from advertising on the site. She then published her first book at the age of sixteen, which has sold over 120,000 copies and, by the time she was nineteen, her business was worth $15 million.

2 Read the text again. Choose the correct answers.

1 Which of these is definitely true?
  a Emil doesn't cut people's grass anymore.
  b Emil is a good student.
  c Emil's business is getting bigger.
  d Emil would make a good teacher.

2 Emil's biggest problem was:
  a not having time to go on dates.
  b giving up other, more pleasurable activities.
  c not being able to sleep properly.
  d not coming from a rich family.

3 Juliette thinks that her website is successful because:
  a she made it for people whose interests she understood.
  b there are lots of different things to do on it.
  c it was well advertised early on.
  d there was nothing like it at the time.

4 One thing Julia does not mention as important for success is:
  a being calm.
  b keeping to your ideas.
  c knowing which people to stay away from.
  d having strong emotions.

Her website is aimed at young teenagers and pre-teens. It has lots of different things on it such as games, advice, music and fashion. This sounds like many other sites for this age group. However, when Juliette had the idea, she was the same age as the target audience and that's why she thinks it became so successful.

Juliette believes calmness is always important to be a success in business, in good times as well as bad. Emotions just get in the way of sensible decision-making. Juliette's final piece of advice is to stick with your ideas. Surround yourself with people who will help to make your ideas succeed and avoid those who cloud your vision by trying to lead you away from where you want to go.

Word Builder Idiomatic language (2)

3 Replace the underlined words with an idiomatic phrase.

1 My parents stopped me going out for two weeks.
My parents grounded me for two weeks.

2 Producing cheap, poor quality goods might make money for a short time but it will damage your business in the future.
Producing cheap, poor quality goods might make money for a short time but it will damage your business in the l_____ r_____ .

3 The website has just had its millionth visitor.
The website has just c_____ u_____ its millionth visitor.

4 No one wanted to help me so I had to organise things on my own.
No one wanted to help me so I had to t_____ m_____ i_____ m_____ o_____ h_____ .

5 It was hard work at first but now that hard work is leading to success.
It was hard work at first but now that hard work is p_____ o_____ .

6 I hope people will hear about my website directly from other people.
I hope people will hear about my website b_____ w_____ o_____ m_____ .

7 Ignore other people's advice. It will just make you less sure about what you are doing.
Ignore other people's advice. It will just c_____ y_____ v_____ .

8 No one else had thought of a website like mine so there was a great opportunity for me.
No one else had thought of a website like mine so the d_____ w_____ w_____ o_____ for me.

Sentence Builder Reference

4 Match the sentences (1-5) with the reference sentences that follow them (a-e).

1 I had six months work experience at a marketing company. _d_
2 I read an article on teen business successes last month. ___
3 We've got a great library in our town. ___
4 Your website is really good. ___
5 My parents' business had a lot of problems last year. ___

a That's why so many people use it.
b That's when I decided to start my own business.
c That's what made me decide not to set up my own business.
d That's how I managed to find a permanent job.
e That's where I found these books on business ideas.

REMEMBER

Complete Exercises A–B before you start this lesson.

A Complete the sentences with the verbs below.

> could borrow   could work   had had   ~~not to ask~~
> not to listen   to concentrate   wasn't going to tell
> was thinking   wouldn't have   wouldn't lend

I decided to set up my own business. When I told people, their reactions were mixed …

1 My parents told me _not to ask_ them for money.

2 My teacher asked me why I _____ about a business just before my exams.

3 She told me _____ on my studies.

4 Tom asked me if he _____ for me.

5 Annie said that I _____ time for her.

6 My brother said that he _____ a better idea than mine.

7 He said that he _____ me what it was.

8 A businessman told me _____ to anyone else.

9 I went to see my bank manager and asked how much money I _____ .

10 He said that he _____ me anything because I was too young.

B Complete the sentences with a verb in the correct form.

1 'What is your name?'
She asked me what my name _was_ .

2 'I'm trying to set up an online shop.'
He said he _____ to set up an online shop.

3 'Where do you work?'
They asked me where I _____ .

4 'Listen to advice from experts.'
She told me _____ to advice from experts.

5 'The business will be a great success.'
She said that the business _____ a great success.

6 'Where have you been?'
My mum asked me where I _____ .

7 'Don't expect to become rich overnight.'
My dad told me _____ to become rich overnight.

8 'I'm going to borrow £2000.'
He said he _____ £2000.

1 * Choose the correct reporting verb.

1 'You should save some money before you try to start a business.'
He ⟨advised⟩/admitted/inquired me to save some money before I tried to start a business.

2 'I don't know what I'm meant to be doing.'
He suggested/admitted/warned not knowing what he was doing.

3 'I can help you if you want.'
He threatened/offered/accused to help me.

4 'How much money do you earn a month?'
They inquired/advised/warned about how much money I earned a month.

5 'If you don't pay back your debts soon, I'll go to the police.'
He accused/warned/threatened to go to the police if I didn't pay back my debts soon.

6 'Your business will do badly if you don't come up with some new ideas.'
My friends warned/threatened/offered me that my business would do badly if I didn't come up with some new ideas.

7 'It would be a good idea to do some work experience.'
He offered/suggested/promised doing some work experience.

8 'You don't care about me.'
She threatened/admitted/accused me of not caring about her.

2 ** Complete the text with the verbs in brackets in the correct form.

When the online shop collapsed, hundreds of people were waiting for products they had paid for. They accused the owner of [1] _stealing_ (steal) their money. The owner promised [2] _____ (pay) them all back but admitted that it [3] _____ (will take) a long time. The customers then threatened [4] _____ (call) the police.

At first, the owner offered [5] _____ (meet) some of the customers but, in the end, his lawyer advised him [6] _____ (not go). The lawyer suggested [7] _____ (go) to the police before the customers did so that's what the owner decided to do. The police inquired about what [8] _____ (happen) and decided that the owner had done nothing wrong. They warned the customers [9] _____ (not do) anything illegal and promised that they [10] _____ (will get) their money as soon as possible. A newspaper journalist then interviewed the owner who admitted [11] _____ (make) a lot of mistakes and said that he [12] _____ (going / look) for a different job.

3 ** Report the conversations from the cues.

Girl: You don't love me.
Boy: I do!
Girl: Will you love me forever?
Boy: Of course I will.

1 She accuse / not love / her
She accused him of not loving her.

2 He / say / he / do

_____

3 She ask / will / love / forever

_____

4 He promise / will

_____

Boss: I don't know what I'm doing.
Secretary: I can help you if you want.
Boss: You're very kind. I wish ...
Secretary: We should work, not talk.

5 He admit / not know / what he / do

_____

6 She / offer / help / if / want

_____

7 He say / she / very kind

_____

8 She suggest / work / not talk

_____

4 *** Complete the second sentence so that it reports the first. Use the words in capitals.

1 I'll finish my homework when I've watched my new DVD. (PROMISED)
She *promised to finish her homework when she had watched her new DVD.*

2 If I were you, I'd talk to a teacher about being bullied. (ADVISED)
My friend _____

3 I lost your camera. (ADMITTED)
Beth _____

4 Do you want me to buy you some bread? (OFFERED)
My mum _____

5 Let's open a shop. (SUGGEST)
My friend _____

6 Be careful of viruses in emails. (US)
They _____

7 You've been wasting my time. (ACCUSED)
She _____

8 Are you planning to start you business this year? (WHETHER WE)
She _____

9 If you don't return our money, Mr Baker, we will write to the local newspaper about your company. (THREATENED)
We _____ our money.

Grammar Alive Impersonal reporting

5 *** Make sentences from the cues.

1 Unemployment / report / reached 2.5 million last month
Unemployment is reported to have reached 2.5 million last month.

2 expect / will go above 3 million next year.

_____

3 the Prime Minister / believe / planning a new scheme to help young people find work

_____

_____

4 Union leaders / know / angry / that the unemployed aren't getting enough help

_____

5 5000 unemployed families / known / lost their homes last year

_____

6 has / said / if nothing is done about the problem / crime / increase in the future

_____

35

Oral Skills

Listening

1 🔊 **2.15** Listen to two people talking and choose the correct answers.

1 Who are the two people?
   businessmen/school students

2 What is the relationship between them?
   friends/business partners

3 What do they call each other?
   first names/surnames/no names

4 What sort of language do they use when talking to each other?
   formal/informal

5 Where are they?
   at work/in a café

6 How are they feeling at the end of the conversation?
   bored/happy

2 🔊 **2.15** Listen again and complete the notes.

1 Lord Sugar is not just a TV __presenter__ .

2 Lord Sugar was born in _____ .

3 One of his ideas was for a cheap

   _____ .

4 Lord Sugar thinks that all prices can be negotiated, even in a _____ .

5 The speakers think about offering less money for their _____ .

6 One boy says that before you start your own business, you need to find a gap in

   _____ .

7 The other boy's idea is to edit people's

   _____ .

8 The business idea wouldn't cost anything because one of the boys has already got

   _____ .

Speaking

1 Match the beginnings (1–8) with the correct endings (a–h).

1 Another thing that's __e__
2 They are made of a special material. That's what ___
3 These jeans are great. What's even ___
4 They are quite cheap. And they do ___
5 All you ___
6 What's brilliant about this shop ___
7 What's also ___
8 But it's the price ___

a is that you can change things even if you lose the receipt.
b need is half a litre of water and it will clean anything.
c better is that you can get two for the price of one.
d makes them so special as they never get dirty.
e fantastic is that they are so easy to use.
f good is that the shop assistants are so friendly.
g that will really shock you.
h have a five-year guarantee.

2 🔊 **2.16** Complete the dialogue with one word in each gap and then listen to check.

A: Look at this box for CDs and games.

B: I don't want to waste my money on that. I want to buy a new game.

A: You really ¹_do_ need something to keep your games in.

B: But it's boring.

A: No, it isn't. ᵃIt's brilliant because it's got special plastic cases for games and DVDs. ᵇIt's also fantastic because it's easy to find what you want quickly. That's ²_____ makes it so great for you because you can never find anything. What's ³_____ better is that it looks cool. I might buy one for myself.

C: Can I help you?

A: We're looking at this box. My brother's interested.

B: No, I'm not. I want a game.

C: Well, this is a very good box. It's very well-made. ᶜBut, most of all, I think you will be amazed by our special offer. If you buy this, you can buy five games or DVDs for the price of three. ᵈThe deal is also good because it lasts for twelve months. So, if you can't afford them now, you can still take advantage of the offer later in the year.

A: Go on, Steve. All you ⁴_____ is £10.

B: Okay, I'll buy it. It'll look good in my room. I'm fed up with the mess in there.

3 Look at the underlined sentences (a–d). Rewrite them by completing the sentences.

a What's brilliant _is that it's got special plastic cases for_
   games and DVDs.

b Another thing _____

   _____

c It's the special _____

d What's _____

36 GRAMMAR
Infinitives

1 * **Match the beginnings (1-10) with the correct endings (a-j).**

1 I may _b_

2 The owner of the shop is reported ___

3 It was the wrong decision ___

4 This fruit has ___

5 Our business doesn't seem ___

6 Some people need ___

7 Paul and Steven don't seem ___

8 You know what you should ___

9 Jack is believed ___

10 It was a good idea to ___

a to be sold before it goes bad.

b have made a mistake.

c to be doing very well at the moment.

d to have been arrested last week.

e to make.

f have done.

g to be told what to do all the time.

h to be trying very hard.

i shop around.

j to have lost all his money because his business failed.

2 ** **Complete the sentences with the correct form of the verbs in brackets.**

1 Suzanne could _have been_ (be) a successful businesswoman if she had wanted.

2 Mr Davies is a good person _____ (ask) for advice.

3 Mr James was arrested yesterday. He is thought _____ (steal) £10,000 from the bank where he used to work.

4 New ways of advertising have _____ (find) because fewer people are reading newspapers.

5 You shouldn't _____ (buy) that shirt in the shopping centre. You could _____ (save) at least £10 if you'd bought it online.

6 Our website seems _____ (have) problems at the moment.

7 I bought these shoes in order _____ (look) smart for my interview.

8 Dan is known _____ (have) help to pass his exams last year.

9 More and more people seem _____ (try) to save money rather than spending so much on luxuries.

10 Paul phoned. He wants _____ (collect) from the cinema at ten o'clock because he hasn't got enough money for a bus.

3 ** **Make sentences from the cues.**

1 This seems / be / popular shopping centre
   This seems to be a popular shopping centre.

2 Everyone / seem / buy / a lot
   _____

3 The prices / seem / lower / since last week
   _____

4 It seem / become / tourist attraction
   _____

5 A lot of improvements / seem / make / since we were last here
   _____

4 *** **Rewrite the dialogues by completing the sentences.**

1 **A:** I think we're going round in circles.
   B: Yes, I didn't turn left at the bank which was a mistake.
   A: We seem _to be going round in circles._
   B: Yes, I should _have turned left at the bank._

2 **A:** No one needs to tell me what to do.
   B: Are you sure? Some people say your team have made a lot of mistakes since you became team leader.
   A: I don't _____
   B: Are you sure? It is said that a lot _____
   _____

3 **A:** I'm going to get a job so that I can save some money.
   B: It's a shame you didn't start looking earlier. There aren't many jobs left now.
   A: I'm going to get a job in order _____
   _____
   B: You should _____ .
   There aren't many jobs left now.

4 **A:** Everyone knows that this shop has put all its prices up recently.
   B: And it seems that a lot of people are shopping in other places.
   A: It is well-known that all the prices in this shop
   _____
   B: And a lot of people seem _____
   _____

5 **A:** I'm glad I have a job.
   B: Well, it's nice when they pay you at the end of the week.
   A: It's good _____
   B: Well, it's nice to _____
   _____

Writing Workshop 9

❶ Read the report and complete the information.

1 Most summer work can be found in t*ourist* r*esorts* .
2 A lot of young people come to England in the summer to i_____ their E_____ .
3 Teachers and s_____ i_____ need special qualifications.
4 To get an unskilled job at a holiday camp, the most important things are the right p_____ and a _____ .
5 You could get work with events such as f_____ and move around the country.
6 Jobs where you have to move around the country often provide f_____ and a _____ .
7 It is important to a_____ e_____ to give yourself a good chance of a job.

Report on summer work in the UK ▶▶

The ¹ *objective* of this report is to look at employment opportunities in the UK during the summer for 18–25 year olds. Not everyone wants to travel abroad and it is possible to find work almost anywhere in the country, ²_____ in the more popular tourist resorts.

Summer camps

Thousands of young people come to England every summer to learn or improve their English. To work as a teacher or sports instructor on a summer camp it is ³_____ to have the relevant qualifications but there are other jobs. You could work as a cleaner or kitchen assistant. Alternatively, if you prefer something a bit more fun, you may be lucky and be taken on as a social organiser, ⁴_____ this is becoming increasingly unlikely as companies cut down on their spending.

Holiday camps

An ⁵_____ is to look for work at holiday camps. They need different kinds of workers, especially those who can help to create a fun atmosphere on the camps. Qualifications are needed for some jobs but many jobs are for unskilled workers and you can get a job ⁶_____ that you have the right personality and attitude.

Other jobs

⁷_____ option providing ⁸_____ you're willing to move around the country is to find work with a festival or a similar event which travels from one place to another. It is important to show a willingness to do whatever is asked and be available twenty-four hours a day. Provided that you are a good worker, you'll be taken all over the country and given free food and accommodation. You should also get a little bit of spending or saving money. It's a great way to see the country and to meet different people. ⁹_____ , it isn't for everyone.

Whatever you choose, it is vital ¹⁰_____ apply early as jobs go fast.

❷ Complete the text with the words (a–j) in the gaps (1–10).

a	alternative	f	objective *1*
b	although	g	particularly
c	another	h	provided
d	essential	i	that
e	nevertheless	j	to

❸ Choose the correct answers.

1 Looking after children is well-paid, _*b*_ it can be very tiring.
 a especially
 b although
 c provided
2 You can work as a security guard ___ you are fit and healthy.
 a particularly
 b nevertheless
 c providing
3 You may need to work in the evening ___ if you are responsible for organising family entertainments.
 a especially
 b providing
 c although
4 The wages aren't very high. ___ , it is possible to save as all meals and accommodation are free.
 a Although
 b Nevertheless
 c Particularly
5 It is ___ to be confident and well organised.
 a essential
 b needed
 c objective
6 Another ___ is to work in the camp restaurant.
 a necessary
 b important
 c option

❹ Write a report about different kinds of work at a holiday camp. Use the headings below.

• The purpose of the report
• Looking after children
• Organising activities for families
• Working in the restaurant
• Security guards

Write between 120 and 180 words.

Check Your Progress 9

1 Business **Complete the sentences with one word in each gap.**

1 I'd like to do some part- ___ work.
2 These products offer good ___ for money.
3 Working as a waiter is a good summer ___ to do.
4 I'd like to get some work ___ as a programmer.
5 I'm interested in doing voluntary ___ .
6 I'm too scared to ___ up my own company.

/6

2 Idiomatic language (2) **Complete the sentences with one word in each gap.**

1 News spread quickly by word of m_____ .
2 You must take m_____ into your own hands.
3 I think you'll make money in the long r_____ .
4 Don't let other people c_____ your vision.
5 I can't go out. I've been g_____ for a week.

/5

3 Reference **Complete the dialogue with the correct reference phrases using** *that's.*

Girl: I'll always remember March 15th.
Boy: Why?
Girl: ¹_____ we met. You were so romantic.
Boy: Was I?
Girl: Of course. ²_____ I fell in love with you. I'll never forget Mario's restaurant.
Boy: Why?
Girl: ³_____ you took me on our first date.
Boy: Did I?
Girl: 'You are like a shining star in a moonlit sky.' ⁴_____ you said to me.
Boy: Are you sure it was me?

/4

4 Reporting **Complete the sentences with the reporting verb in capitals.**

1 'You left the door unlocked all night.' (ACCUSE)
My boss _____
2 'I won't forget to phone again.' (PROMISE)
Sylvia _____
3 'I'll tell your parents if you're late again.' (WARN)
My teacher, Mrs Austin, _____
_____
4 'If I were you, I'd go on a cookery course.' (ADVISE)
My friend _____
5 'I like Lady Gaga's records.' (ADMIT)
My brother _____

/5

5 Reporting **Use the beginnings to paraphrase each sentence in two ways.**

People expect prices to rise quickly next year.
1 Prices are _____
2 It is _____
Economists believe that this company is having problems.
3 It is _____
4 This company is _____
Everyone knows that house prices were too high last year.
5 It is _____
6 House prices are
_____

/6

6 Infinitives **Complete the second sentence so that it paraphrases the first.**

1 I think they are lost.
They seem _____
2 I think someone has told them to leave.
They seem _____
3 I think they are locking the doors.
They seem _____
4 I think these cameras are used to watch the shop assistants, not the customers.
These cameras seem _____
_____

/4

TOTAL SCORE /30

Module Diary

1 **Look at the objectives on page 85 in the Students' Book. Choose three and evaluate your learning.**

1 Now I can _____
well / quite well / with problems.
2 Now I can _____
well / quite well / with problems.
3 Now I can _____
well / quite well / with problems.

2 **Look at your results. What language areas in this module do you need to study more?**

Sound Choice 5

Sound Check

Say the words and expressions below.

a What you should do is … , That's what I told her to do, Young people are believed to be … (Exercise 1)

b join, shingle, arch, vision (Exercise 2)

c accept, secondly, nature (Exercise 3)

d colour, organise, likeable (Exercise 4)

e sociable, efficient, picturesque, update (v), record (n) (Exercise 5)

2.17 Listen and check your answers. Which sounds and expressions did you have problems with? Choose three exercises to do below.

1 **2.18** Grammar - sentence stress **Listen to the sentences and repeat the** underlined **phrases. Then make your own sentences using the** underlined **phrases and say them aloud.**

1 What you should do is phone him and apologise.

2 That's what I told her to do.

3 I can't understand what he's saying.

4 Young people are believed to be more willing to move away from home to find work than in the past.

5 It is often said that Venice is the most beautiful city in Europe.

6 The number of people out of work is reported to have reached three million.

2 **2.19** Consonants - /dʒ/, /ʃ/, /tʃ/ and /ʒ/ **Complete the table with the words below and then listen to check.**

arch beige butcher cheap
gorge imagine ~~join~~ multinational
publish shingle vision

	Beginning of the word	Middle of the word	End of the word
/dʒ/	¹ join	2	3
/ʃ/	4	5	6
/tʃ/	7	8	9
/ʒ/		10	11

3 **2.20** Vowels - /ə/ **Look at the words. Write the correct letter (B, M or E) depending on whether the schwa sound /ə/ comes at the beginning of the word (B), in the middle of the word (M) or at the end of the word (E). Then listen and repeat the words.**

1 accept _B_
2 secondly ___
3 nature ___
4 nation ___
5 waterfall ___
6 company ___
7 outlets ___
8 internet ___
9 agree ___
10 amaze ___

4 **2.21** Spelling - British and American English **Look at the spelling differences. Then listen to the words and write them in American and British English.**

British	American
colour	color
1 _____	_____
2 _____	_____
theatre	theater
3 _____	_____
4 _____	_____
organise	organize
5 _____	_____
6 _____	_____
likeable	likable
7 _____	_____
8 _____	_____

5 **2.22** Difficult words - word stress with adjectives **Complete the table with the words below in the correct column. Then listen to check.**

sociable beautiful survive efficient
record (n) impressive update (v) marvellous
present (n) increase (v) picturesque wonderful
survival disappear human

Ooo	oOo	ooO	oO	Oo
sociable				

TOPIC TALK – VOCABULARY

❶ Replace the definitions in brackets with one word in each gap.

This is an extremely ¹s*imple* (not complicated) but ²o_____ (completely new and different to anything else) design. It looks ³c_____ (fashionable and expensive) and very ⁴s_____ (attractive in a fashionable way). This sort of design is very ⁵t_____ (influenced by the most fashionable styles and ideas) at the moment, which means that people are willing to pay a lot for it.

The good thing about this shirt is that the material is very ⁶d_____ (staying in good condition for a long time, even if used a lot) because it is so well-made. It is also ⁷e_____-f_____ (does not harm the environment when it is made or when you use it) as it is made from natural, organic cotton. It is very ⁸p_____ (useful or suitable for a particular purpose or situation) and can be worn for working in the garden or a night out at the theatre.

I wouldn't recommend this mobile phone. It looks very ⁹o_____-f_____ (not considered to be modern or fashionable any more) and it is quite ¹⁰i_____ (not sensible or possible for practical reasons). The phone is poor quality and doesn't work ¹¹p_____ (correctly, or in a way that is considered right).

❷ Complete the clothes adjectives with one letter in each gap.

Opinions
¹e *l* e *g a* n *t*   ²c _ _ u _ l
³o _ _ r _ g _ _ _ s

Fit
⁴b _ g _ _   ⁵t _ _ h _

Style
⁶s _ _ _ t-s _ _ _ v _ d
⁷r _ _ n _ -n _ _ k _ d

Material
⁸w _ _ l   ⁹d _ _ _ m

Pattern
¹⁰s _ _ _ p _ d   ¹¹p _ _ _ n
¹²f _ _ w _ _ y

❸ Label the pictures with the correct words from Exercise 2.

He is wearing
¹ _*casual*_ (opinion),
² _____ (fit),
³ _____ (material) jeans.

She is wearing an
⁴ _____ (opinion),
⁵ _____ (style),
³ _____ (pattern) dress.

❹ Complete the text with the words below.

break cheap conscious dated fortune last lasting
~~look~~ looks made object rebellious useless what

Michelle, aged 15
I think clothes should ¹ _*look*_ striking and a bit ² _____ – you know, something that parents won't like. ³ _____ I don't like are clothes which are boring.

Dan, aged 16
My favourite ⁴ _____ is my laptop because it ⁵ _____ stylish and it is long-⁶ _____ and well-⁷ _____ .

Emma, aged 14
My dad is not at all fashion-⁸ _____ . He wears terrible shirts. They are very ⁹ _____ and old-fashioned and, what's worse is that they cost a ¹⁰ _____ !

Alex, aged 17
I don't understand why everyone wants one of these phones. They ¹¹ _____ easily and they don't ¹² _____ long. They are totally ¹³ _____ but they aren't at all ¹⁴ _____ – in fact they are quite expensive.

37

GRAMMAR
Regrets

REMEMBER

Complete Exercises A–B before you start this lesson.

A Complete the second sentence so that it has the same meaning as the first. Use the word in capitals.

1 It is possible that this is Carole's phone. (COULD)
   This _could be_ Carole's phone.

2 We are forced to wear a tie to school. (HAVE)
   We _____ a tie to school.

3 I'm sure this price is wrong. (MUST)
   This _____ wrong.

4 My advice is to keep the receipt safe. (SHOULD)
   You _____ the receipt safe.

5 This scarf only cost £5. I'm sure it isn't real silk. (CAN'T)
   This _____ silk. It only cost £5.

6 It's possible that this old vase is worth a lot of money. (MAY)
   This old vase _____ a lot of money.

7 It isn't necessary to get changed before you go out. (HAVE)
   You _____ before you go out.

8 If you drop your MP3 player, it is possible that it will break. (MIGHT)
   If you drop your MP3 player, _____ .

B Complete the dialogues with the phrases below.

> had to walk   ~~must be~~   must be
> must have broken   must have forgotten
> should have taken   shouldn't have done

A: Your phone ¹ _must be_ very well-made.
B: I know, I'm always dropping it.

A: My MP3 player was useless so I threw it away.
B: You ² _____ that. You ³ _____ it back to the shop.

A: Whose is this T-shirt?
B: It ⁴ _____ Tom's. He was playing tennis earlier. He ⁵ _____ it.

A: You look tired.
B: I am. I ⁶ _____ home. The bus didn't come. It ⁷ _____ down.

1 * Complete the sentences with the correct form of the verb in brackets.

1 **A:** You _____ _could have got_ _____ (could / get) those shoes cheaper online.

2 **B:** Really? I _____ (should / ask) you which websites to look at.

3 **A:** Elaine _____ (could / win) that race.

4 **B:** I know. She _____ (should / train) harder.

5 **A:** You _____ (should / wear) something warmer.

6 **B:** I know. I _____ (should / check) the weather forecast before I came out.

7 **A:** There's Emma. She _____ (could / buy) us a ticket, too.

8 **B:** We _____ (could / be) at the front of the queue if you'd woken up earlier.

2 ** Complete the sentences with the verbs below in the correct form.

be   can   have   ~~not spend~~

I spent all my money yesterday. Now, I'm broke. I haven't got any money and I can't buy these cool jeans.

1 I wish I _hadn't spent_ all my money yesterday.
2 I wish I _____ some money today.
3 I wish I _____ buy these jeans.
4 I wish I _____ broke.

ask   be   not buy   read

I bought a new camera last week. I didn't read the instructions and the photos I took at Monica's party weren't very good. That's why I deleted them all from my computer.

5 I wish I _____ the instructions.
6 I wish I _____ someone else to take the photos.
7 I wish the photos _____ better.
8 I wish I _____ this camera so soon before the party.

3 ** Complete the dialogues with the correct form of the verbs in brackets.

A: Come on. The shops are going to shut soon.
B: I wish [1] _they stayed_ (they / stay) open all night. They do in some countries.

A: That was a lovely pizza. I wish [2] _____ (I / order) a large one now.
B: You're kidding! I wish [3] _____ (I / not eat) so much. I feel really full.

A: I wish [4] _____ (you / not have to) go home now.
B: So do I but I must do some studying. I wish [5] _____ (I / understand) the maths we've been doing recently.
A: I know what you mean. I wish [6] _____ (the exams / be) over and [7] _____ (we / be) on holiday already.

A: I wish [8] _____ (my computer / not be) so slow.
B: It's all those free programmes you've downloaded.
A: I know. I wish [9] _____ (I / not download) anything. They all sound so good, though.

A: Andy scored five goals for the school football team yesterday.
B: Wow. I wish [10] _____ (I / see) that.

4 *** Complete the wishes about the information given.

1 I'm not a designer but I'd like to be one.
I wish _____ _I was a designer._ _____
2 I haven't got a Saturday job but I'd like one.
I wish _____
3 I bought these trousers but I don't like them.
I wish _____
4 I can't play the guitar but I'd like to.
I wish _____
5 I broke my mum's vase.
I wish _____
6 I didn't go to the party. I was bored at home.
I wish _____
7 I haven't got anything cool to wear.
I wish _____
8 We live in a small town - there's nothing to do.
I wish _____
9 I was rude to Jane yesterday which I regret.
I wish _____

Grammar Alive Expressing regrets

5 *** Make sentences from the cues.

A: I like your trousers.
B: [1]wish / try on / in / shop
I wish I had tried them on in the shop.
A: Why?
B: They're too tight. [2]wish / be / five kilograms lighter.
_____
A: [3]wish / I / slim as you
_____
A: How's your new phone?
B: It's okay but [4]wish / have / iPhone
_____
A: My parents gave me an iPhone for my birthday. [5]wish / they / not buy it.
_____
B: Why?
A: I'm too scared to take it to school in case it gets broken or stolen.
A: Do you like your new house?
B: Not really. [6]wish / we / not move
_____
A: Why?
B: The area is really boring. [7]wish / be / more to do here.
_____

103

1 Read the text. Match the paragraphs (A–G) with the gaps in the text (1–6). There is one extra paragraph.

A At first, they would be used for short journeys where high speeds are not necessary. They could be used as a cheap second car, keeping a traditional car for longer journeys, although Nègre hopes to be able to find a replacement for these, too.

B They may not have to. There are still many problems to overcome before the dream becomes a reality. Meanwhile, Nègre continues his work.

C The main reason is that other fuels are very polluting. Petrol is the worst. A mixture of battery power and petrol is only slightly cleaner. Hydrogen is very expensive and electrical cars rely on inefficient or unreliable battery power.

D These will include all sorts of cars from three-wheelers to a five-door family saloon. There could even be buses and boats. That depends on demand, of course, and whether anyone will buy the cars.

E When Nègre discovered this, he didn't give up. Instead it made him even more determined to succeed. Back at the factory he made a new discovery.

F Nègre certainly knows what he is talking about. He has spent over the last ten years developing compressed air technology near Nice in the south of France. At his factory, it is possible to test the cars.

G If the pump for the air is powered by clean energy, then the car will be 100% pollution-free. And, as has been said before, even if its performance is improved by using petrol, it will still be far less polluting than most cars.

Guy Nègre

Guy Nègre is a French automobile designer. One of his greatest designs is the cheap, environmentally-friendly Air Car. It runs on air and, even though it can only reach speeds of 50 kph at the moment, it could be the start of a new era in car design. So why did he decide on air as a fuel?

1 _C_

Can the car succeed? Nègre believes it can. It is cheaper than an electric car, doesn't have batteries that need replacing every five years and is much quicker to recharge.

2 ___

In the factory car park, the cars work well. Even if they aren't as comfortable as normal cars, it has to be remembered that these are just test cars, not the final models. When they go on sale, Nègre hopes that there will be more choices available.

3 ___

There has already been some interest from the airline Air France KLM. They are thinking of using the air cars to replace their electric cars at Amsterdam's Schiphol Airport. As technology improves, the cars could be used for different purposes.

4 ___

To do this, he is also working on a car which combines both air and petrol power. Negre says that this will be ultra-efficient and be able to travel hundreds of kilometres on one litre of petrol. That will make it very environmentally friendly.

5 ___

However, even though there would be obvious benefits to both the environment and customers, the car still hasn't been seen on our roads. It is unknown when it will become available. Are petrol companies deliberately preventing its production?

6 ___

He may be overambitious. His dream may never come true. Even so, no one can accuse him of not trying.

2 **Read the text again and choose the correct answers.**

1 Guy's cars would be:
   a faster than existing cars.
   b cleaner than existing cars.
   c cheaper than existing cars.
   d more reliable than existing cars.

2 Guy has lots of experience of working with:
   a air power.
   b fossil fuels.
   c electric power.
   d hydrogen power.

3 The cars that you can test drive:
   a are on sale now.
   b are being used at Amsterdam Airport.
   c include many different kinds of car.
   d are not the same as the cars that will be sold.

4 Guy may produce air-petrol hybrid cars because they would be:
   a cleaner than air-powered cars.
   b better for longer journeys than air-powered cars.
   c more comfortable than air-powered cars.
   d cheaper than air-powered cars.

Word Builder Prefixes

3 **Choose the correct prefixes in each sentence.**

1 The engine is very *in/un*efficient.
2 If the pilot is here with us, the plane must be flying on *ultra/auto*pilot.
3 He's a great designer but I think this project may be a little *over/ultra*ambitious.
4 We got a *pre/re*view of the new engine. We were the first people in the world to see it.
5 How long does it take to *re/over*charge the battery in this camera?
6 Sorry, but that name is completely *un/in*known to us.
7 We *under/over*estimated how much food we needed. It's all gone and the party only started an hour ago.
8 This kitchen is *ultra/auto*modern. It's like stepping into the twenty-second century.

4 **Complete the sentences with a prefix and the correct form of the words in capitals.**

1 I'm not trying to ___*reinvent*___ the car. I'm trying to invent something completely new. (INVENT)
2 The buses were always _____ and you couldn't move at all. (CROWDED)
3 Our library is _____ . Some days no one goes in there at all. (USED)
4 Henry Ford was the first to mass produce the _____ . (MOBILE)
5 You could borrow a car at a special car park which has a _____ battery. You then take it back at the end of the day. (CHARGED)
6 If someone invented an _____ car then people would drive even faster than they do now. (CRASHABLE)
7 I feel quite _____ when I go to a party and don't know anyone. (SECURE)
8 This engine is _____ and will work much better than any engine ever made before. (EFFICIENT)

Sentence Builder *even*

5 **Complete the sentences with the phrases below. You can use each phrase twice.**

> even if   even so   even though

1 I wouldn't drive one of these cars ___*even if*___ you bought it for me.
2 It still hasn't been produced _____ they have been working on it for twenty years.
3 It's a great idea. _____ , there are some problems.
4 I'd love one. _____ , I don't think it is worth $10,000.
5 People still use their cars too much _____ they know that it is bad for the environment.
6 _____ air cars work well, I don't think they'll become as popular as petrol cars for another twenty years.

Listening

1 **2.23** **Listen to an interview about problems with sat-nav and decide how the stories are organised (1–4).**

1 Chronologically (i.e. when they happened).
2 To illustrate different types of problem with sat-nav.
3 In order of how bad the problems were.
4 By country.

2 **2.23** **Listen again and choose the correct answers.**

1 The Swedish tourists made a mistake because:
   a they didn't realise Capri is an island.
   b there are two places called Capri in Italy.
   c they wrote the wrong place name in their sat-nav.

2 Hampton Court Palace is:
   a in the centre of London.
   b to the south-west of London.
   c in north London.

3 The problem with the road in Crackpot is that:
   a it isn't suitable for normal cars when the weather is bad.
   b there are no warning signs.
   c you often get stuck behind slow-moving tractors.

4 The guest on the show:
   a had problems when he tried to go to Lille.
   b knew how to get to Lille before he set off.
   c reached his destination without using sat-nav at all.

5 The problem the tourists had going to Lille was caused by the same thing as:
   a the Swedish tourists' problem.
   b the problem the schoolchildren had.
   c the problem drivers have on the road in Crackpot.

Sentence Builder *It's time …*

3 **Rewrite the sentences in two different ways using *It's time* and the verb forms in brackets.**

You should have a rest.
1 (have) _____ *It's time to have a rest.* _____
2 (had) _____ *It's time you had a rest.* _____
We should get sat-nav for our car.
3 (get) _____
4 (got) _____
They should put up a sign to warn drivers not to drive here.
5 (put) _____
6 (put) _____
We should buy a better map.
7 (buy) _____
8 (bought) _____
I should find a new job.
9 (find) _____
10 (found) _____

Speaking

1 **Complete the sentences with the correct form of the words in brackets.**

1 So what do you think the problem ____*is*____ (be)?
2 This light keeps _____ (flash).
3 That _____ (can) be the cause of the problem but I doubt it.
4 What do you think is the _____ (good) thing to do.
5 The problem with _____ (do) that is that it might cause more problems than it solves.
6 _____ (other) option would be to check for ideas on the internet.

2 **2.24** **Complete the dialogues with one word in each gap. Then listen to check your answers.**

1 A: This light on my computer ¹k*eeps* flashing. What do you ²t_____ the problem is?
   B: It ³m_____ be a problem with the battery.

2 A: ⁴W_____ I try to open this programme, the computer goes blank. What do you think is the ⁵b_____ thing to do?
   B: One ⁶s_____ would be to uninstall the programme and then try to install it again.

3 A: Let's take the back off and have a look inside.
   B: The problem ⁷w_____ doing that is that we don't really know what we're looking for.

4 A: Shall we save everything onto these USB flash drives and then reinstall Windows and start again?
   B: ⁸M_____ , but it might take a long time to do that. Another ⁹o_____ would be to take it to the shop and ask them to look at it.

LESSON

40 GRAMMAR Modality

1 * **Choose the correct words.**

1 You really *ought to*/*are obliged to* see this film. It's great.

2 We *didn't have to*/*were forbidden to* do the last exercise because we'd worked so hard.

3 You are *required to*/*allowed to* pay for the course in advance. If you don't pay, you won't be *required to*/*allowed to* attend.

4 They *forced us to*/*had to* stand in the rain for twenty minutes. We were really wet when we got home.

5 We bought the boat so we *should*/*could* go fishing.

6 Do I *need to*/*obliged to* fill in everything on this form?

7 You are only *forbidden to*/*permitted to* leave early if you have a note from your parents.

8 We *had to*/*need to* leave at six o'clock tomorrow morning.

2 ** **Complete the word and then put the verb in brackets into the correct form.**

If you want to buy clothes worn by some of Hollywood's top entertainers, then you'll ¹n*eed* *to* *spend* (spend) a lot of money. Not surprisingly, Marilyn Monroe's dresses have been some of the most expensive. One of the cheapest is the dress she wore in the film *Gentlemen Prefer Blondes*. The person who bought that ²h_____ _____ _____ (pay) $310,000 in 2010, which was cheap compared to the dress she wore when she sang 'Happy Birthday' to President Kennedy in 1962. That cost $1.26million in 1999. The person who bought that ³s_____ _____ _____ (wait) eleven years then, they ⁴c_____ _____ _____ (buy) the dress from *Gentlemen Prefer Blondes* instead and still had $950,000 left to spend on something else!

It wouldn't have been enough to buy the white dress that Marilyn Monroe wore in *The Seven Year Itch*, though. $5.6 million was ⁵r_____ _____ _____ (purchase) that in 2011 and it is still the most expensive dress ever. Not surprisingly, excited buyers were ⁶f_____ _____ _____ (touch) the dress before the sale.

However, if these prices are shocking, perhaps you ⁷o_____ _____ _____ (sit) down before reading on. In 2011, Elizabeth Taylor's jewellery was sold. The person who bought her famous 'La Peregrina' necklace ⁸h_____ _____ _____ (spend) $11.8 million and the whole collection cost an incredible $116 million!

3 ** **Look at the signs and make sentences from the cues.**

> **Do not touch the dresses**

1 It / forbid / touch / the dresses
   It is forbidden to touch the dresses.

2 You / permit / touch / the dresses
   _____

> **Do not leave your bags unattended. Thieves operate in this museum.**

3 You / ought / have / money belt
   _____

4 You / should / leave / bags / unattended
   _____

> **The museum closes at 6p.m.**

5 We / have / leave / by 6 p.m.
   _____

6 We / allow / stay / after 6 p.m.
   _____

7 We / require / leave / by 6 p.m.
   _____

4 *** **Complete the second sentence so that it has the same meaning as the first. Use the word in capitals.**

1 You should be more careful. (OUGHT)
   You *ought to be more careful.*

2 You don't have to buy anything. (OBLIGED)
   You _____

3 It's important that you recharge your mobile phone. (NEED)
   You _____

4 No one is saying that you have to come. (FORCING)
   No one _____

5 You're not allowed to go out on your own. (FORBIDDEN)
   You _____

6 Can we try these dresses on? (ALLOWED)
   Are _____

7 It was possible for people to take photos of the dress. (COULD)
   People _____

8 They didn't let us stay for the auction. (PERMITTED)
   We _____

Writing Workshop 10

1 **Read the letter quickly and decide which advert it is in response to.**

Advert ___

A

Modelling school in Paris.
Two week courses in July and August.
Look good, feel great and learn a lot.
Expert help and guidance.
€500 for a two week course.
Accommodation not included.
Contact: Mr Davies

B

DESIGN AND TECHNOLOGY COURSE IN BRISTOL

July 18th–August 1st.

Some computer skills will be required.

Group and project work as well as individual tutoring.

Course fees £500.

Contact: Mr Davies

Dear Mr Davies,

I am writing ¹_____ ask you for more information about your summer courses which I saw advertised online.

First of all, I would like to know whether I am suitably qualified. I have been on a one-week hairstyling course and a two-week clothes design course. I am very interested in a career in the fashion industry one day. ²_____ , I would like to take a course ³_____ I can have something to show potential employers in the future.

Another query I have is related to accommodation. This is not mentioned at all in your advert and, ⁴_____ , I'm not sure whether I would be expected to find somewhere for myself or if accommodation is provided at an extra charge. I'd like to know quite early ⁵_____ I can start looking for somewhere to stay if necessary ⁶_____ I don't know anyone in the Bristol area.

My last question is about social events ⁷_____ I think it would be nice to have a chance to get to know the other students outside the classroom situation. Could you send me details of any extra activities or excursions to look at?

I look forward to hearing from you soon.

Yours sincerely,
Kate Swinton

K Swinton

2 **Choose the words below that can be used in the gaps (1-7) in the text. Sometimes more than one option is possible.**

1	**a** in order to	**b** so that	**c** because
2	**a** As	**b** Therefore	**c** So that
3	**a** so that	**b** so	**c** because
4	**a** therefore	**b** since	**c** as a result
5	**a** so	**b** in order to	**c** so that
6	**a** since	**b** as	**c** so
7	**a** therefore	**b** as	**c** because

3 **Complete the sentences with one word in each gap. Sometimes more than one word is possible.**

1 I am interested in the course _as/since/because_ I would like to be a designer when I leave school.

2 I am not sure about the price of the course. _____ , I would be grateful if you could send me full details of how much the course costs.

3 I am writing this letter in _____ to ask you for more information about your summer courses.

4 I would be grateful if you could let me know the dates of the courses so _____ I can make plans for the summer.

5 I have already agreed to work during July and, as a _____ , would only be able to attend a course in August.

6 I have an aunt who lives in London _____ I will not need you to find me accommodation.

7 I would like to attend the course _____ learn more about design and technology.

8 I would be grateful for more details of the course content _____ I have been on similar courses and would like to know whether this one will offer anything new.

4 **Imagine you are interested in the other course from Exercise 1. Write a similar letter to the one above using the information below:**

- You've never done any modelling work but you are interested in doing so.
- You can only go in July as you are working in August.
- You'd like more details of what is included.
- You'd like to know if you can have help with finding accommodation and, if so, how much it is likely to cost - you don't know anyone in Paris and would like to share a flat with someone else from the course if possible.
- You'd like to know if there are any trips organised to see Paris as you have never been there before and would love to have some time to see famous landmarks.

Write between 150 and 200 words.

Check Your Progress 10

1 Design Complete the phrases with one word in each gap.

1 It's such a great product because it is so up-to-d_____ .
2 This mobile phone is very user-f_____ .
3 I hope this computer is longer-l _____ than my old one.
4 Most of the clothes they sell here are very well-m_____ .
5 Don't you think that this dress looks a bit old-f_____ ?
6 I prefer round-n_____ jumpers because they keep you warmer.
7 You should wear short-s_____ shirts in the summer.
8 I'm not very style-c_____ but I know what clothes suit me.

/8

2 Regrets Complete the sentences with the correct form of the verbs in brackets.

1 I wish I _____ (not be) so tall.
2 Your shirt's got a hole in it. You should _____ (buy) something more durable last week.
3 I wish the shop _____ (have) more summer dresses when I went there last week.
4 I wish you and I _____ (be) the same size then I could borrow your clothes.
5 You could _____ (tell) me that these phones didn't work properly before I bought one.
6 I wish these shoes _____ (not look) so cheap.

/6

3 Prefixes Complete the sentences with the prefixes below.

in   over   pre   re   un   under

1 I'm not completely _____known. The local paper published a story about me last year.
2 This club is so small that it is _____crowded when there are more than ten people in it.
3 This is a really _____efficient way to produce energy.
4 You can't _____charge these batteries. You'll have to buy some new ones.
5 The local council wants to close our club because it is _____used.
6 There was a special _____view of the film last week and everyone said it was very good.

/6

4 It's time Complete the second sentence so that it means the same as the first. Use the word in capitals.

1 We need to talk. (WE)
It's time _____
2 Stop writing. It's home time! (TO)
Stop writing. It's time
_____
3 You should do your homework now. (YOU)
It's time _____
4 My shoes need replacing. (I)
It's time _____
5 We have to leave now. (TO)
It's time _____

/5

5 Modality Choose the answer which is **wrong**.

1 It wasn't necessary for us to leave so early.
We _____ leave so early.
a didn't have to   b weren't allowed to
c didn't need to
2 You can't sit here.
You _____ to sit here.
a are required   b are forbidden
c aren't permitted
3 You are required to wear a uniform.
You _____ to wear a uniform.
a are forced   b are permitted   c have
4 My advice is to wear this dress.
You _____ wear this dress.
a are allowed to   b ought to   c should
5 It was possible to hear him from far away.
We _____ hear him from far away.
a could   b were able to   c ought to

/5

TOTAL SCORE   /30

Module Diary

1 Look at the objectives on page 95 in the Students' Book. Choose three and evaluate your learning.

1 Now I can _____
well / quite well / with problems.
2 Now I can _____
well / quite well / with problems.
3 Now I can _____
well / quite well / with problems.

2 Look at your results. What language areas in this module do you need to study more?

Exam Choice 5

Reading

1 Read the text. Match the paragraphs (A–G) with the gaps in the text (1–6). There is one extra paragraph.

A One of the main difficulties was persuading people that the car was safe. It was very low which made it difficult for other drivers to see it. It was also very slow which would make it difficult to avoid cars that were coming too close.

B Of course, it did have advantages, too. One was that drivers didn't need a driving licence to take it onto the roads. It was also very cheap.

C He had first started to think of such a vehicle when he was a teenager. However, work was delayed by his concentration on computers and calculators in the 1970s.

D In fact tests showed that it wasn't as dangerous as some people feared. However, it was just one of many reasons why people's opinions about the car tended to be negative.

E In October 1985, the Hoover Company announced that it was going to stop producing the car. It looked as if Sir Clive's dream had finished forever.

F It was at about this time that problems started to appear. One was that the car was made by the Hoover Company, which more famous for selling household appliances.

G One of the most famous failures in recent British business history was the launch of the C5. This was a small, electric vehicle that was launched in 1985 by Sir Clive Sinclair.

Many experts agree that launching a successful new product is one of the most difficult things to do in business. So many things can go wrong that it is amazing that anyone manages to do it.

¹___ He had already had some business success with his personal computers which he had been selling for just £100, much less than the normal selling price of £500. The idea of producing an electric car was not new for Sir Clive. ²___ Another reason for the delay was that he had to wait until his small, electric vehicle was practical. Improvements in the batteries needed to power the car helped. A change in the law in 1983 also made production of the car possible. ³___ This led to the story that the cars were powered by a washing machine engine. It wasn't true but it was the first of many problems Sir Clive had with the public's opinion of his cars. ⁴___ Not only that, it had no roof which meant that it could only really be used for half of the year and then only on sunny days. It also had difficulties in getting up steep hills. ⁵___ Its price wasn't enough to persuade people to buy it, however. Although Stirling Moss, a famous Formula 1 driver, was used in adverts for the car, only 17,000 were bought. ⁶___ However, in 2010, he gave a newspaper interview in which he said that he was working on a new car. This was called the X-1 and he hoped that it would be on sale by 2011. That date came and went but, perhaps, one day, Sir Clive will see a successful launch of his electric car.

2 Read the text again. Decide whether the sentences are true (T), false (F) or if there is no information (NI).

1 The C5 was the first electric car in Britain. ____
2 Sir Clive's computers were cheaper than most computers at the time. ____
3 Hoover were well-known for their cars before they started making the C5. ____
4 The cars used the same engine as a washing machine. ____
5 One thing that people were worried about was the height of the car. ____
6 The car had a roof which could be removed on sunny days. ____
7 The people who bought the car weren't happy with it. ____
8 The X-1 first went on sale in 2011. ____

Listening

3 **2.25** Listen to someone talking about the businessman Gerald Ratner and complete the sentences with one or two words in each gap.

1 Gerald Ratner was born in _____ .
2 He was thirty-four years old when he took over his _____ .
3 By the time he was forty, Gerald Ratner had made Ratners the biggest _____ in the world.
4 The speech he made was to the Institute of _____ .
5 When one of his directors read his speech, he suggested adding some _____ .
6 Ratner compared a pair of earrings to a _____ .
7 There were _____ people watching his speech.
8 After the speech, the business did badly and Ratner _____ .
9 He found success again with a fitness club which he sold for just under _____ pounds in 2001.

Speaking

4 Complete the dialogue with one word in each gap.

Examiner: In the next part of the exam, I'd like you to discuss this problem. Here you have some electrical items but you can only take one of them on holiday with you. I'd like you to discuss the advantages and disadvantages of each and try to decide which one to take. You have three minutes for this task.

Student A: Well, let's start with the laptop. In my opinion, it's the worst option. The problem ¹_____ that it is too heavy.

Student B: Yes, but it ²_____ have a big screen. What's great ³_____ a laptop is that you can watch films if you're bored. Another ⁴_____ that's brilliant is that you can put all your films and songs onto the hard drive with no problem.

Student A: Maybe, but if we were on holiday, it ⁵_____ be better to spend the time meeting people or seeing the sights, not watching films in our hotel room. I think ⁶_____ we need is a way of contacting people and accessing the internet.

Student B: Okay. So, what do you think is the ⁷_____ thing to take?

Student A: The mobile phone. It's got everything, don't you think so?

Student B: Well, the problem ⁸_____ taking a phone is the cost. I've read about people who come home from their holidays and they find a bill for thousands of pounds. It might happen to us.

Student A: It's possible but I doubt ⁹_____ . We know about this and wouldn't make the same mistake. One solution would ¹⁰_____ to have a prepaid charge. When you use all your money you can't make phone calls or use the internet.

Student B: Then it would be useless!

Student A: What do you suggest?

Student B: Well, ¹¹_____ option would be to take the netbook. It's smaller than the laptop but we could use Skype to contact people.

Exam Choice 5

Use of English

5 Complete the text with the correct form of the words in capitals.

Until a few weeks ago, I had a temporary job working for a large ¹_____ (NATIONAL) company in their design team. Unfortunately, I lost my job last month. The boss said I was ²_____ (RELY) because I took a few days off but I had a doctor's note so it was a bit unfair. I don't think he liked me because I look quite ³_____ (REBEL) with my leather jacket, spiky hair and ⁴_____ (COLOUR) T-shirts.

I'm now doing ⁵_____ (VOLUNTEER) work for a clothes company. It's a great place to work. They make ⁶_____ (ENVIRONMENT)-friendly clothes and they have asked me to design some T-shirts. That's great because I'm quite ⁷_____ (CREATE) and one of the things I disliked about my old job was that my skills were ⁸_____ (USED) because the boss didn't trust me. He was totally ⁹_____ (USE) at his job really. I think he only got it because his uncle worked there. He was worried that someone more talented than him would be given his position. That's why we were ¹⁰_____ (FORBID) to attend design meetings. He pretended our ideas were his.

Writing

6 Read the advert. Then complete the sentences with one word in each gap.

> ### Learn Italian in Italy
> We offer a three-week course in July and in August.
> Four hours of lessons every day.
> Four different levels for all abilities.
> Accommodation included in the price.
> Organised activities to make your stay more enjoyable.
> We can arrange to meet you at the airport if you wish (*extra charge applies).
> Write now for more details or to ask for our full colour brochure.

1 I am writing to you i_____ o_____ t_____ ask for more information about the Italian language courses advertised on your website.

2 I have never studied Italian before. T_____ , I would need a course for complete beginners.

3 Is the accommodation with a family? I would like to live with an Italian family a_____ it would give me lots of practice of the language.

4 Could you tell me what you mean by 'organised activities'? Would there be any excursions? I would be very interested in visiting some of Italy's famous cities b_____ I am fascinated by its history and culture.

5 I would only be able to attend the August course s_____ our school summer holidays don't start until the end of July.

6 I haven't travelled much on my own and, a_____ a r_____ , I would feel happier if someone could meet me at the airport and take me to my accommodation.

7 Would you be able to send me your brochure s_____ t_____ I can read more about the course and other information?

8 Would I need a laptop t_____ study on in the evenings?

7 Write a letter asking for more details about the Italian language course in the advert using the information below.

- You are an advanced level student – are there courses for you?
- You don't need accommodation – would there be a discount?
- You don't need to be met but would like a map showing where the school is.
- You have an Italian friend, who you will stay with. Is it possible for him/her to come to the activities? He/She is happy to pay.

Write between 150 and 200 words.

Sound Choice 6

Sound Check

Say the words and expressions below.

a I could've bought … , He should've got … , I wish I'd been there. (Exercise 1)

b gone, finger, bag, sing (Exercises 2 and 3)

c fewer, mayor, dial (Exercise 4)

d school, catch, light (Exercise 5)

e It might be a problem. One solution would be … , The problem with doing that is … (Exercise 6)

f preview, unknown, underused (Exercise 7)

2.26 **Listen and check your answers. Which sounds and expressions did you have problems with? Choose three exercises to do below.**

---

❶ **2.27** **Grammar - contractions** Write the word which contains a contraction in each sentence. One word contains two contractions.

1 _could've_   5 _____
2 _____   6 _____
3 _____   7 _____
4 _____

❷ **2.28** **Consonants - /g/** Listen and repeat the words.

1 gone
2 gadget
3 game
4 elegant
5 finger
6 burgundy
7 baggy
8 flag
9 bag
10 beg
11 blog

❸ **2.29** **Consonants - /ŋ/** Write the words which include the letters *ng* together. Write - if the word doesn't include the letters *ng* together. Listen again and repeat the words.

1 _thing_   7 _____
2 __-__   8 _____
3 _____   9 _____
4 _____   10 _____
5 _____   11 _____
6 _____   12 _____

❹ **2.30** **Vowels - /juːə/, /eɪə/, /aɪə/, /əʊə/ and /aɪə/** Look and listen to the words in the list. Then listen to five more words and write them next to the words with the same vowel sounds. Listen again to check and repeat the words.

/juːə/	fewer	_____
/eɪə/	layer	_____
/aɪə/	dial	_____
/əʊə/	shower	_____
/aɪə/	fire	_____

❺ **2.31** **Spelling** Listen and write the words. Write the number of letters in each word.

1 _school (6)_   6 _____
2 _____   7 _____
3 _____   8 _____
4 _____   9 _____
5 _____   10 _____

❻ **2.32** **Expressions** Listen and <u>underline</u> the stressed word in each sentence. Then listen again and repeat the sentences.

1 It <u>might</u> be a problem.
2 One solution would be to lower the price.
3 The problem with doing that is that we haven't got much time.
4 That could be the cause of the problem but I doubt it.
5 That might work but we won't know for sure until we test it.
6 Maybe, but it might take a long time to do that.

❼ **2.33** **Difficult words** Listen to the words below. Write them in the correct column and <u>underline</u> the stress.

preview unknown recharge underused
overambitious corduroy V-necked old-fashioned
long-lasting ostentatious autopilot
style-conscious uncrashable knee-length

The first syllable is stressed		A different syllable is stressed	
<u>pre</u>view		un<u>known</u>	

FREEDOM FIGHTERS

Task: Find out about a freedom fighter.

Tools: www.infoplease.com/biography/var/aungsansuukyi.html
www.pitara.com/magazine/people/online.asp?story=35
simple.wikipedia.org/wiki/Aung_San_Suu_Kyi
en.wikipedia.org/wiki/Aung_San_Suu_Kyi
www.nobelprize.org/nobel_prizes/peace/laureates/1991/kyi-bio.html

Skills: Finding information about people, evaluating websites, writing a short personal profile.

Before you start

1 **Look at the photo of Aung San Suu Kyi and read her profile. <u>Underline</u> three facts you think might not be true.**

Aung San Suu Kyi was born in 1945. Her father negotiated independence from the British but was assassinated when she was only two. Her mother was an ambassador and Aung San Suu Kyi lived in India before going to Oxford University. After working at the UN in New York, she married Dr Michael Aris and had two children. In 1988, she returned to her country to look after her mother and started the National League for Democracy with a non-violent campaign for political freedom. She won the elections in 1990 but the military government took power and put her under house arrest for 15 years. She has received wide international support and won the Nobel Peace Prize in 1991.

Research

2 **Choose three of the websites in Tools. Check the information in Exercise 1 and correct the three facts that are not true. Then write notes about two of these things.**

- Her childhood and family background
- Her studies and travels
- Her entry into politics
- Her fight for freedom

3 **Evaluate the three websites you used. Which:**

1 was the easiest to understand? ___

2 had the best information? ___

3 was best organised? ___

4 looked the most reliable? ___

Tip!

When evaluating websites in English to get information, think about these things.

- The level of language: websites for young people or simplified websites can have more accessible language, e.g. Simple English Wikipedia.
- The amount of information: depending on the kind and amount of information you need you should use different types of websites, e.g. for basic information, use simple websites.
- The organisation of the websites: is it easy to find the contents? Are there summaries of information? Is there a search facility?
- Reliability: is the information up-to-date? Is it from a reliable source, e.g. a well-known encyclopedia? Does it give further references or links?

Task

4 **Choose another freedom fighter, e.g. Nelson Mandela. Write notes about these things.**

- Childhood/family
- Studies/work/travel
- Entry into politics
- Fight for freedom
- Results of fight

Tip!

It is easier to search using the English version of Google. Look for <u>Google.com in English</u> at the bottom of each Google search page. When you want to find basic information about a person using Google, put their name in quotation marks and add other words: *"Nelson Mandela" + very short/brief biography* or *"Nelson Mandela" + quick facts/information.*

5 **Write a short profile of a freedom fighter like the profile of Aung San Suu Kyi in Exercise 1. Use your notes from Exercise 4.**

Review

In this task I have:

- researched information about famous people.
- evaluated websites.
- written a short profile about a famous freedom fighter.

TV ADVERTS

Task:	Watch a TV advert and evaluate it.
Tools:	Online award-winning adverts:
	1 www.britisharrows.com/award/john-lewis/ or www.youtube.com/watch?v=pSLOnR1s74o
	2 www.britisharrows.com/award/bbc-tv-radio-station-promotions-2/ or www.youtube.com/watch?v=auSo1MyWf8g
	3 www.britisharrows.com/award/renault-ze-vehicles-automotive-products/ or www.youtube.com/watch?v=pJGzF57_EMQ
Skills:	Searching for TV adverts and comparing and evaluating them.

Before you start

1 **What do you think makes a good TV advert? Put the criteria (a–f) in order.**

a Information about the product and why it is special ☐
b Human interest and a good story ☐
c Strong visual impact and good photography ☐
d Humour and thought-provoking content ☐
e Songs and background music ☐
f Memorable dialogues and slogans, e.g. *LG - Life's Good* ☐

Research

2 **Watch the three prize-winning adverts in the links in Tools. Choose the best summary (a–c) of each advert's main message.**

1 a Our shop has the best Christmas offers.
  b At our shop we care about people.
  c People can't wait to get presents from our shop.

2 a We have the best nature documentaries.
  b We care about the world's wildlife.
  c We work to protect nature.

3 a Petrol engines are no good for most machines.
  b Petrol engines are noisy and pollute a lot.
  c Electric power is the cleanest and most convenient form of energy.

3 **Watch the adverts again and give them marks out of five for each of the criteria (a–f) in Exercise 1.**

1 a *3/5* b *4/5* c ___ d ___ e ___ f ___
2 a ___ b ___ c ___ d ___ e ___ f ___
3 a ___ b ___ c ___ d ___ e ___ f ___

Task

4 **Search for two 30-seconds or one-minute TV adverts of similar products that are not offensive, rude or stereotypical. Write notes on these things about each advert.**

- What it is selling/promoting
- Its main message
- Its characters and storyline
- How it gets across its message, e.g. music/photography/humour
- Why it is effective/not so effective

Tip!
When searching for TV adverts, you can use the main Google search page or search directly in YouTube. Use the 'plus' and 'minus' options on both Google and YouTube to get adverts you want and to avoid adverts that you do not want, e.g. *TV adverts +clothes +computers -cars -beer -shampoo -football.*

5 **Work in groups. Use your notes to tell the other students about your two adverts and to compare them.**

My two adverts are for soft drinks. In the first advert, there's a guy jogging along a road when … In the second advert, a family is watching TV at home when … I think the first advert is better because it is funny and it is …

Review
In this task I have:
- watched and evaluated TV adverts.
- searched for TV adverts.
- described and compared two TV adverts.

FILMS

Task: Find out about a film using a film website and trailer.
Tools: www.imdb.com/title/tt1515091/
Skills: Using a film website to get information, watching trailers to get impressions of films.

Before you start

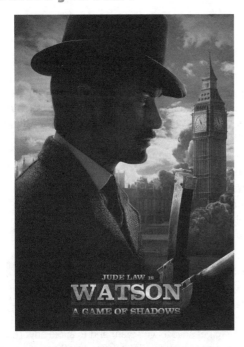

JUDE LAW is
WATSON
A GAME OF SHADOWS

① **Which of these things most influence your decision to watch a film?**

a   The trailer

b   What friends say about it

c   Information on websites, e.g. about the actors

d   Film reviews

Research

② **Go to www.imdb.com/title/tt1515091/, the film website of *Sherlock Holmes: A Game of Shadows*. Put the things (a-f) in the order they come in the website.**

a   Frequently asked questions ☐

b   Information about financial success ☐

c   The title and basic information (year/classification/length/genre/rating) *1*

d   Quotes from the film ☐

e   Reviews of the film ☐

f   Storyline: plot summary ☐

③ **Go to the user reviews of the film again. Click on <u>See all user reviews</u> ». Use the filter to choose one good review (Loved it) and one bad one (Hated it). List reasons the reviewers give.**

Loved it: great action

Hated it: Robert Downey Jr not like Sherlock Holmes

④ **Watch the trailer twice and order these scenes.**

a   Sherlock Holmes and Watson at home with a dog barking ☐

b   Sherlock Holmes and Watson fighting ☐

c   Watson describing Sherlock Holmes's behaviour and recommending a sedative ☐

d   Sherlock Holmes and a woman dancing *1*

e   Sherlock Holmes pushing a woman off a train ☐

⑤ **Write notes about your impressions of the film from the website (information/reviews/trailer). Use these headings.**

- Type of film
- Director/stars
- Good characters?
- Clever/funny dialogue?
- Interesting/exciting scenes?
- Good photography/music?

Task

⑥ **Choose another film from www.imdb.com. Read the information about it and two reviews. Then watch the trailer. Write notes using the headings in Exercise 5.**

Tip!

Watch the film trailers twice with no sound to get an idea of the content first. Then watch it with the sound. Use the counter at the bottom to repeat parts that you want to watch again. Go to the quotes section of the website. The quotes can help you understand dialogue in the trailer.

⑦ **Use your notes to write a short report about the film.**

It's an action film called … directed by … The scenes look exciting, especially …

⑧ **Work in pairs and tell your partner about your film.**

Review

In this task I have:

- used a film website to get information.
- read film reviews to get people's opinions.
- watched a film trailer to get an impression of a film.
- written a short report and talked about a film.

TRAVEL PLANS

Task: Plan a trip to a famous tourist attraction.

Tools: 1 simple.wikipedia.org/wiki/Machu_Picchu

2 www.peru-machu-picchu.com/

3 www.tripadvisor.co.uk/Attraction_Review-g294321-d668949-Reviews-Machu_Picchu-Urubamba_Sacred_Valley_Cusco_Region.html

Skills: Finding information from different websites and using it to make travel plans.

Before you start

1 Look at the photo of Machu Picchu. What do you know about it? What else would you like to know? Write three questions.

I know: It's in Peru. It was built ...

Question 1: How can you get there?

Research

2 Read about Machu Picchu at simple.wikipedia.org/wiki/Machu_Picchu. Try to answer your three questions from Exercise 1.

3 Go to www.peru-machu-picchu.com/. Look at the map and choose four things to visit. For each of them, read the information and click on click here for virtual tour. Use the pan and zoom tools to explore and then write notes about each place.

Funerary Rock Hut - great views

> **Tip!**
> Use an online dictionary to look up the meaning of words you do not know, e.g. www.ldoceonline.com/dictionary/tomb
>
> **tomb** [countable]
> a stone structure above or below the ground where a dead person is buried:
> 🔊 the family tomb

4 Look at ten visitor reviews at www.tripadvisor.co.uk/Attraction_Review-g294321-d668949-Reviews-Machu_Picchu-Urubamba_Sacred_Valley_Cusco_Region.html. Find practical information about these things.

- When to go
- How to get to the area
- Where to stay
- How to get to the ruins
- Worth hiring a guide?
- Other things worth doing in the area, e.g. hikes

Task

5 Choose another historic place to visit. Go online and find basic information, photos and visitor reviews. Write notes about the place and the things in Exercise 4.

> **Tip!**
> When you want to visit a place, first of all find out basic information about it, e.g. using a website like Simple English Wikipedia. Decide if you really would like to go there. Go on a virtual tour of the place if one is available. Finally, look at visitor reviews and comments, e.g. on www.tripadvisor.co.uk to get useful travel tips. Make sure you read at least ten reviews to get a balanced idea of the place.

6 Use your notes to write a travel plan to the place you have chosen.

7 Work in groups. Tell the other students about your travel plans. Which trip would most of the group like to do?

I'm going to go to Stonehenge. I'm going to stay the night in Salisbury because it's a lovely city. Then I'm going to take an early bus and ...

> **Review**
> In this task I have:
> - **found out information about places using different kinds of travel websites.**
> - **used the information to write travel plans and talk about them.**

INVENTIONS

Task: To find out about inventions and give a short talk.

Tools: didyouknow.org/history/radiohistory/
answers.yahoo.com/question/index?qid=1005121401223
curiosity.discovery.com/question/who-invented-the-radio
inventors.about.com/od/rstartinventions/a/radio.htm
science.howstuffworks.com/innovation/inventions/who-invented-the-radio.htm
www.pbs.org/tesla/ll/ll_whoradio.html

Skills: Evaluating websites, getting information from different websites, checking and comparing facts.

Before you start

Tip!
When looking for information about a topic, do not just use one website. Choose at least three that have clear information and which are not too complex. Choose websites that look reliable, with up-to-date information and references to sources of information. Take notes from each website. Then compare your notes and check inconsistencies. If you are still not sure about a fact, check it on the other websites.

3 Who would you call the 'father of the radio', Marconi or Tesla?

4 Choose another invention and find out about it. Write notes from three different websites about these things.
- Previous discoveries that influenced it
- When it was invented
- Who invented it (one person or various scientists)
- When it was first used
- How it was improved/developed
- What impact it had on everyday life

1 Look at the photo and the questions (1–3). Try to guess the answers.

1 Who invented the radio?
  a the Italian scientist Marconi
  b the Serbian scientist Nikola Tesla
  c various scientists contributed to its invention

2 What was Tesla's most important contribution?
  a he invented a machine transmitting radio waves
  b he discovered the existence of radio signals
  c he demonstrated the practical applications of radio

3 What was Marconi's most important contribution?
  a he invented a new machine for transmitting and receiving radio waves
  b he discovered the existence of radio signals
  c he demonstrated the practical applications of radio

Task

5 Use your notes to prepare a short talk about your invention.

The first calculators were abacuses and then in the 17th century simple mechanical calculators were invented. In the 19th century, Charles Babbage produced the first complex mechanical computers.

Review
In this task I have:
- found information from different websites.
- checked and compared facts.
- talked about an invention.

Research

2 Choose three of the websites in Tools to answer the questions in Exercise 1. Then decide which of the facts (1–5) are true (T) and which are false (F).

1 Tesla sent a radio signal 50 miles in 1895. ___
2 Marconi's first experiments with radio communication were in 1895 in Italy. ___
3 Marconi's first radio transmission in 1896 was based on Tesla's and other scientists' work. ___
4 Marconi got public recognition for inventing the radio. ___
5 Before he died, Tesla won the battle with Marconi to patent the radio in the USA. ___

Topic Wordlist

COUNTRY AND SOCIETY

communities
abandoned (adj)
be off (v)
boarded-up (adj)
bond (n)
burnt-out (adj)
celebration (n)
community service (n)
cultural diversity (n)
decent (adj)
efficient (adj)
favela (n)
heavy traffic (n)
hierarchy (n)
hospitality (n)
housing (n)
inhabitant (n)
lock (v)
make camp (phrase)
overcrowded (adj)
privacy (n)
sense of community (n)
slum (n)
solidarity (n)
tribesman (n)

crime and law
bandit (n)
brutally (adv)
capture (v)
conflict (n)
Constitution (n)
corruption (n)
court case (n)
cruel (adj)
cruelty (n)
curfew (n)
defiance (n)
gang (n)
investigate (v)
key witness (n)
legal action (n)
outlaw (v)
persecution (n)
riot (n)
sinister (adj)

slaughter (v)
spy (n)
thug (n)
unjust (adj)
untrue (adj)
vandalism (n)

international conflicts
anti-missile system (n)
attack (n)
defeat (v)
nuclear weapon (n)
tank (n)

landmarks
aqueduct (n)
arch (n)
be located (v)
breathtaking (adj)
burial site (n)
column (n)
dome (n)
enormous (adj)
extraordinary (adj)
eye-catching (adj)
intact (adj)
interior (n)
magical (adj)
marble (n)
marvellous (adj)
panel (n)
picturesque (adj)
pyramid (n)
rectangular (adj)
round (adj)
stained glass (n)
statue (n)
stone circle (n)
striking (adj)
unforgettable (adj)
unsupported (adj)
walkway (n)

places
chain store (n)
club (n)
corner shop (n)
department store (n)
dock (n)
harbour (n)

hypermarket (n)
salon (n)
stadium (n)

politics
approve (v)
banner (n)
boycott (n)
cut (n)
donate (v)
fundraising (n)
go on (v)
healthcare (n)
issue (n)
liberty (n)
petition (n)
principal (adj)
public spending (n)
radical (adj)
scandal (n)
segregation (n)
society (n)
tactics (n)
undemocratic (adj)

religion
god (n)
offering (n)
theology (n)

social issues
animal testing (n)
awareness (n)
closely-knit (adj)
equal (n)
inequality (n)
infant mortality (n)
life expectancy (n)
mid-income (adj)
NGO (n)
racial (adj)
sanitation (n)
second-class citizen (n)
suicide (n)
take a stand (phrase)
xenophobic (adj)

CULTURE

art and literature
chapter (n)
fiction (n)
fine art (n)

artists
folk singer (n)
pianist (n)
rapper (n)

mass media
celebrity (n)
coverage (n)
distort (v)
dumb down (v)
exaggerate (v)
flash (n)
glamour (n)
icon (n)
iconic (adj)
over react (v)
panic (n)
power (n)
tabloid (n)
the press (n)
trashy (adj)
trivial (adj)
universal (adj)
update (n)
weekly (adj)

music
concerto (n)
freestyle (v)
gig (n)
grime (n)
hybrid (n)
improvise (v)
label (n)
mainstream (adj)
masterpiece (n)
promo (n)
unsigned (adj)

television and radio
broadcast (v)
chat show (n)
concept (n)
current affairs (n)
duo (n)
game show (n)
listener (n)
mockumentary (n)
news bulletin (n)
parody (n)
phone-in (n)
podcast (n)
radio (n)
radio station (n)
satire (n)
sitcom (n)
spoof (n)
voiceover (n)
wacky (adj)

FAMILY AND SOCIAL LIFE

daily routine
alarm clock (n)
do things (v)
hectic (adj)
midday (n)
midnight (n)
table manners (n)

family life
adopt (v)
be descended from (v)
childless (adj)
cohabit (v)
matriarchal (adj)
orphaned (adj)
parental authority (n)
remarry (v)
separated (adj)
trend (n)
widow (n)
widower (n)

family members
ancestor (n)
birth parent (n)
extended family (n)
first cousin (n)
grandchild (n)
great-grandfather (n)
great-grandmother (n)
lone parent (n)
second cousin (n)
third cousin (n)

leisure time
hang around (v)
hang out (v)
interests (n)
summer camp (n)

FOOD

food items
beetroot (n)
citrus fruit (n)
grape (n)
pomegranate (n)

HEALTH

healthcare and treatment
acupuncture (n)
alternative medicine (n)
anaesthetic (n)
check-up (n)
consulting room (n)
curable (adj)
herbal medicine (n)
holistic (adj)
homeopath (n)
homeopathy (n)
lotion (n)
pharmaceutical (adj)
practitioner (n)
prescribe (v)
preventable (adj)
proof (n)
scientific (adj)
side effect (n)
therapist (n)
vaccinate (v)

healthy/unhealthy lifestyle
anabolic steroid (n)
antioxidant (adj)
cholesterol (n)
deplete (v)
far-reaching (adj)
herbal tea (n)
long-term (adj)

natural (adj)
stamina (n)
UV radiation (n)

illness/injury
alcoholism (n)
bruise (v)
cancer (n)
chickenpox (n)
cholera (n)
chronic (adj)
cold (n)
collapse (n)
constipation (n)
exhausted (adj)
fatigue (n)
graze (v)
heart attack (n)
heart disease (n)
hepatitis (n)
lactic acid (n)
measles (n)
meningitis (n)
migraine (n)
mumps (n)
pull a muscle (phrase)
rabies (n)
rash (n)
salmonella (n)
sinusitis (n)
sprain (v)
strain (v)
stroke (n)
TB (n)
tear (v)
tumour (n)
typhoid (n)

parts of the body
collarbone (n)
head (v)
kidney (n)
ligament (n)
liver (n)
lung (n)
rib (n)
tendon (n)

sports science
accumulate (v)
breakdown (n)

capacity (n)
contraction (n)
haemoglobin (n)
intense (adj)
performance-enhancing (adj)
physiology (n)
rate (n)
tissue (n)

describing houses
brick (n)
entrance (n)
garage (n)
shutter (n)
wheelbarrow (n)
wooden (adj)

NATURAL ENVIRONMENT

animals
antelope (n)
bonobo (n)
cheetah (n)
coyote (n)
herd (n)
offspring (n)
penguin (n)

environmental issues
conservation (n)
decay (v)
deterioration (n)
exposure (n)
global warming (n)
nuclear reactor (n)
pesticide (n)

landscape
bay (n)
coniferous (adj)
deciduous (adj)
estuary (n)
fjord (n)
glacier (n)
gorge (n)
grassland (n)
moorland (n)
pampas (n)

pass (n)
pasture (n)
peak (n)
prairie (n)
savanna (n)
seafront (n)
shingle (n)
spring (n)
steam (n)
steppe (n)
track (n)
treacherous (adj)
tundra (n)

natural disasters
bury (v)
catastrophe (n)
destruction (n)
eruption (n)
famine (n)

natural science
characteristic (n)
context (n)
desirable (adj)
disperse (v)
distant (adj)
natural selection (n)
reproduce (v)
tendency (n)
transform (v)

PEOPLE

appearance
baldness (n)
solid (adj)
strike (sb) (v)

clothes
halter dress (n)
waistband (n)
walking shoes (n)

clothes adjectives
beige (adj)
bizarre (adj)
burgundy (adj)
checked (adj)
classy (adj)

close-fitting (adj)
corduroy (n)
cream (adj)
crimson (adj)
dated (adj)
different (adj)
feminine (adj)
loose (adj)
masculine (adj)
ostentatious (adj)
outrageous (adj)
pleated (adj)
scarlet (adj)
simple (adj)
sophisticated (adj)
striped (adj)
stylish (adj)
trendy (adj)
turquoise (adj)
velvet (n)
V-necked (adj)
wool (n)

describing people

absent-minded (adj)
alpha male (n)
altruism (n)
ambitious (adj)
analytical (adj)
anxious (adj)
arrogant (adj)
articulate (adj)
assertive (adj)
athletic (adj)
bad-tempered (adj)
biker (n)
bright (adj)
centre of attention (n)
courageous (adj)
cynical (adj)
dedicated (adj)
defiant (adj)
desperate (adj)
determined (adj)
dreamy (adj)
driven (adj)
eccentric (adj)
empathy (n)
expressive (adj)
fault (n)

fearless (adj)
feminist (n)
frown (v)
giggle (v)
good-natured (adj)
grin (v)
hedonist (n)
height (n)
hospitable (adj)
humorous (adj)
indifferent (adj)
industriousness (n)
irresponsible (adj)
irritable (adj)
likeable (adj)
logical (adj)
meticulous (adj)
modest (adj)
mysterious (adj)
nosy (adj)
on edge (phrase)
opinionated (adj)
over-tired (adj)
pallid (adj)
pessimistic (adj)
preoccupied (adj)
punctual (adj)
reckless (adj)
reclusive (adj)
reserved (adj)
rude (adj)
sceptical (adj)
self-confident (adj)
self-esteem (n)
selfish (adj)
single-minded (adj)
snobbish (adj)
stable (adj)
stupid (adj)
sympathetic (adj)
thoughtful (adj)
vegan (n)
warm (adj)
welcoming (adj)
well-educated (adj)
witty (adj)
yawn (v)

relationships

be fond of sb (v)
be in love (v)
best friend (n)
break up (v)
chat up (v)
chat-up line (n)
dump (v)
get on with (sth) (v)
get to know sb (v)
have a laugh (v)
have a row (v)
have sth in common (with) (v)
not give a damn (phrase)
opposite (n)
partner (n)
put family first (phrase)
put sb off (v)
see sb (v)
single (adj)
speed date (n)
split up (v)
take sb/sth for granted (v)
trust sb (v)
unmarried (adj)

SCHOOL

people and places

canteen (n)
classmate (n)
classroom (n)
corridor (n)
professor (n)

school life

A level (n)
calculator (n)
curriculum (n)
deadline (n)
excursion (n)
expectations (n)
GCSE (n)

SCIENCE AND TECHNOLOGY

inventions
automated (adj)
collision avoidance system (n)
overambitious (adj)
over-engineer (v)
pre-charged (adj)
recharge (v)
reinvent (v)
sensor (n)
uncrashable (adj)
underestimate (v)
wackiness (n)

space/universe
Martian (n)
meteorite (n)

technology
3G (adj)
airbrush (v)
app (n)
chip (n)
computer terminal (n)
computer-manipulated (adj)
crash (v)
cylinder (n)
diesel (n)
flash (v)
gear (n)
glitch (n)
high definition (adj)
hydraulic (adj)
interference (n)
internal combustion engine (n)
LCD (n)
overheat (v)
pen drive (n)
power supply (n)
pressurise (v)
processor (n)
provider (n)
rocket (n)
software (n)
speedy (adj)

sundial (n)
velocity (n)

using the internet
connectivity (n)
cursor (n)
file sharing (n)
phishing (n)
reboot (v)
search engine (n)
social media (n)
spyware (n)
video sharing (n)
wall (n)
wiki (n)

SHOPPING AND SERVICES

advertising
advertisement (n)
agency (n)
billboard (n)
bombard (v)
brand (n)
circulate (v)
commercial (n)
covert advert (n)
creativity (n)
critical (adj)
direct mail (n)
dramatic (adj)
endorsement (n)
exclusive (adj)
influence (v)
junk mail (n)
market (v)
marketer (n)
pop-under (n)
pop-up (n)
product review (n)
promote (v)
sexist (adj)
spam (n)
sponsor (v)
target (v)

targeted ad (n)
tasteless (adj)

goods
aftershave (n)
appealing (adj)
classic (adj)
cult object (n)
disadvantage (n)
durable (adj)
environmentally friendly (adj)
facility (n)
first impression (n)
functional (adj)
futuristic (adj)
glove (n)
hi-fi (system) (n)
impractical (adj)
in (good/perfect/bad etc) shape (phrase)
innovative (adj)
light (adj)
must-have (adj)
sleek (adj)
tacky (adj)
tripod (n)
unoriginal (adj)
unsafe (adj)
up to date (adj)
useless (adj)
user-friendly (adj)
washing powder (n)
well-made (adj)

selling/buying
consumer protection (n)
inefficient (adj)
inexpensive (adj)
overpriced (adj)
price tag (n)
satisfaction (n)
satisfactory (adj)
service (n)
value for money (phrase)
vending machine (n)
window shopping (n)

SPORT

sports people
elite (adj)
first-rate (adj)
motivate (v)
top-level (adj)
top-ranking (adj)
uncoordinated (adj)
world record (n)
world-class (adj)

TRAVELLING AND TOURISM

air travel
airplane (n)
boarding pass (n)
cabin crew (n)
stewardess (n)

transport
automobile (n)
carriage (n)
engine (n)
motorcycle (n)
petrol (n)
racing car (n)
railway (n)
subway (n)
taxi (n)
utility vehicle (n)
vehicle (n)

WORK

business
a gap in the market (phrase)
acquire (v)
apprenticeship (n)
brainstorm (v)
chairman (n)
competition (n)
conference (n)
controversial (adj)
dollar (n)
entrepreneur (n)
fire (v)
generate (v)
grounding (n)
inflation (n)
input (n)
intuition (n)
investment (n)
judgment (n)
link (n)
loan (n)
market research (n)
media mogul (n)
multinational company (n)
network (n)
potential (adj)
prototype (n)
public relations (n)
quirky (adj)
retailer (n)
revenue (n)
shares (n)
snap decision (n)
sponsored (adj)
strategy (n)
tycoon (n)
union (n)
unique selling point (n)
visionary (n)

describing jobs and skills
ambition (n)
applicant (n)
day job (n)
employee (n)
monitor (n)
self-employed (adj)
semi-professional (adj)
studio (n)
unpaid (adj)
unsuitable (adj)
voluntourism (n)
workload (n)
youth unemployment (n)

job market
full-time (adj)
interview (n)
pay and conditions (n)
unemployment (n)

jobs
architect (n)
civil servant (n)
firefighter (n)
forest ranger (n)
historian (n)
horseman (n)
instructor (n)
interpreter (n)
mathematician (n)
microbiologist (n)
philosopher (n)
physicist (n)
programmer (n)
shepherd (n)
stockbroker (n)
theologian (n)
volcanologist (n)

Exam Choice Audioscripts

Exam Choice 1, Listening, Exercise 3

1 Hi, it's Emma here. Sorry I haven't phoned before. How are you? How are mum and dad? I hope everything's okay. The main reason I'm phoning is that I'm hoping to come and visit you all at the weekend. I've had a cold but I'm feeling better now. I really want to see Dad and apologise for missing his 60th birthday. I should have remembered. I've seen the photos on Facebook. It looks as if you had a good time.

2 My mum's really angry with me today. Last week was her 50th birthday party which was a great day. I had a brilliant idea for her present and she was very pleased. It was a weekend in Venice! I showed her the photos from the party which I put on Facebook. She was happy until she realised that my dad is one of my Facebook friends. Since the divorce she doesn't want him to see what she's doing with her life at all.

3 My parents are divorced and my dad now lives in the USA. I don't mind. My boyfriend's parents are divorced, too. It's easy to keep in touch with Dad on Facebook and I like looking at the photos of his new family. The main problem is that he wants me to go there as often as possible. I can't go during the school year and my mum always wants to spend the holidays with me. Sometimes it's difficult to know what to do for the best.

4 My problem is that I had an argument with my girlfriend today. It was her birthday and I took her to a nice restaurant but she'd read an article about heart attacks and didn't want to eat anything unhealthy. I didn't mind that but she wanted me to have a salad as well instead of steak and chips. I made a joke about her coming to visit me in hospital and she walked out. Now I'm sitting looking at her Facebook page and wondering if I should contact her.

5 I love my Facebook page which I've had for a few years now. It was great when I was in hospital to be able to get messages from friends. Even my parents like it and it isn't often that they both agree on something! Now, a friend has started writing a blog. He's very interested in the environment so his blogs are about campaigns and protests. I'd love to have a blog, too. The problem is I just don't know what to write about. It's really annoying me.

Exam Choice 2, Listening, Exercise 3

John: Hi, Amy. Would you like to read the newspaper?

Amy: Hi, John. Is there anything interesting in it?

John: Not really. I didn't read much. There was something about problems with the euro, education in England and Arsenal losing to Milan at football.

Amy: Don't you read it all?

John: I haven't got time. I read it on the bus to school. My dad always asks me to get it for him so he can read it in the evening. Do you read a newspaper?

Amy: I read loads but I never buy any. I read them online.

Matt: You read what online?

Amy: Hello, Matt. I read online newspapers.

Matt: Oh, they are a waste of time. They don't publish the truth. You should read blogs and other websites. Find out what's really going on in the world.

Amy: Matt, the websites you read don't tell you the truth. You were telling me about aliens in Scotland last week!

Matt: It's true. Of course, the government have told the newspapers to keep it quiet. They don't want anyone to know.

John: You're crazy, Matt. So, Amy do you watch the news on television?

Amy: I do sometimes but only because my mum and dad always watch it. I enjoy the twenty-minute news programme at ten o'clock. I can't stand the 24-hours-a-day news channels, though.

John: Why not?

Amy: You just see the same bit of film over and over again. It's so boring.

John: I don't think you're meant to watch them for long. They're good to find out what's going on whenever you like. Then you can switch off again. What do you think, Matt?

Matt: The television is worse than the newspapers. What you think is the news is all filmed in a studio. Everyone you see is just acting.

Amy: Matt, I really think you should take a break from those websites for a few weeks.

Exam Choice 3, Listening, Exercise 3

Good morning, ladies and gentlemen. Welcome to the Laurel and Hardy Museum. Before we go inside, I'd like to tell you a little about Stan Laurel, a true comedy genius. He was born on 16th June 1890, here in this village. His name wasn't really Stan Laurel, though. He was born Arthur Jefferson, that's J-E-F-F-E-R-S-O-N. He enjoyed acting from an early age and, in 1910, he joined a group of young actors on a tour of the USA. Stan later got a career in silent films, earning $75 a week.

By 1926, Stan had decided that he wanted to give up acting and become a writer and director. However, another actor working for the studio had an accident so Stan was asked to return to acting. The other actor was Oliver Hardy and, when he had recovered, he and Stan joined together to become one of the most popular comedy teams of all time. Soon afterwards, silent films were replaced by talkies and many actors failed to make the change from one kind of film to the other. If you have seen the 2012 Oscar-winning film *The Artist* you'll know what I mean. Laurel and Hardy, though, were perfect in talking pictures and became hugely successful in the 1930s.

Unfortunately, war, age and illness brought their careers to an end. In the 1950s, both men had strokes and Stan decided to retire. He lived the rest of his life in Santa Monica, California. His phone number and address were in the local telephone directory so he spent much of his time answering letters and phone calls from fans.

At the age of 74, Stan had a heart attack. In hospital a few days later, he told the nurse that he would like to go skiing. When she asked him if he was a keen skier, he replied that he wasn't but said 'I'd rather be doing that than this.' Those were his final words – a comedian right until the end.

Now let's go inside and see the museum.

Exam Choice

Exam Choice 4, Listening, Exercise 3

1 We went to Bratislava in Slovakia. I really liked it. It wasn't as crowded as Prague. What I really liked was the New Bridge. I thought it was an amazing sight. There is a restaurant high up at the top of a kind of tower but it was closed when we were there. It's a shame because I'm sure there would have been a nice view.

2 I went to Colmar in France. It was very pretty although I don't remember any really obvious landmarks. Just old houses. There wasn't much to do there. Most of the tourists we saw were happy to eat and drink in the town square and walk along the river. It was perfect though because all the waiters and shop assistants we talked to were so warm and hospitable. I'd love to live there.

3 Arundel is a very small town near the south coast of England. It's only got a population of about 3000 but I didn't want to leave because I had such a good time! We played golf, went fishing, went to a nature reserve, looked round the castle, went shopping, swam in the local pool and saw some concerts in the evening. The locals were also very friendly and sociable – it was the perfect holiday!

4 I've always wanted to see the Trevi Fountain in Rome. We went in February so I thought it would be quiet there but you couldn't move! I couldn't take any photos because there was always someone blocking the view. In the end, we walked to some nearby shops and bought some postcards of the fountain. It was the only way to see the view clearly!

5 We went to the south-east of Germany, south of Dresden. The area is full of strangely shaped rocks. The area is so big that it was easy to escape from the crowds. In one place, there was a bridge high up in the hills which crossed a gorge. You could see the river far below and more hills and rocks in every direction. It was an amazing sight and I took a lot of photos.

Exam Choice 5, Listening, Exercise 3

Gerald Ratner isn't the best businessman in the world but he is one of the most famous. He is the businessman who told the world that his products were rubbish.

Gerald Ratner was born in north London and had left school with no qualifications. He took over his family's business in 1984 when he was just 34 years old. At the time, the business owned 100 shops but they weren't doing very well. Gerald proved to be an excellent businessman. By the time he was forty, Ratners was the biggest jeweller's in the world with 2500 shops. At the age of 41, he was asked to make a speech to the Institute of Directors at the Royal Albert Hall in London. Before the evening, he showed the speech to one of his directors who said that it was okay but perhaps it needed a few jokes.

So, Gerald Ratner made a joke. It was about a silver drinks tray with six glasses that his company sold for £9.95. 'Why is it so cheap?' he asked. 'Because it's total rubbish.' He then continued the joke saying that the company sold a pair of gold earrings for less than the price of a sandwich. He went on to say that the sandwich would probably last longer than the earrings. At the time, Gerald Ratner thought the speech would stay private between himself and the five thousand people in the audience. Unfortunately, a daily newspaper heard about the speech and told the world what he had said. The company lost most of its customers and Ratner was sacked from his own family business.

Other business ideas failed until he opened a fitness club. He offered free membership and five hundred people joined. He then went to the bank to borrow some money and was able to tell them that his club had five hundred members. He sold the business in 2001 for almost four million pounds and he's now got an online business – selling jewellery.

Exam Choice and Online Skills Answer Key

Exam Choice 1

1 C
2 1 NI 2 T 3 T 4 F 5 F 6 T 7 NI 8 T
3 1 d 2 e 3 a 4 c 5 f
4 1 c 2 b 3 b 4 c 5 a
5 1 opinion 2 Personally 3 afraid 4 agree 5 sorry 6 true 7 clear 8 convinced
6 1 for 2 to 3 so 4 had 5 As 6 of 7 up 8 from 9 any 10 few 11 been
7 1 c 2 f 3 a 4 d 5 b 6 e
8 Students' own answers

Exam Choice 2

1 1 b 2 d 3 e 4 c 5 a
2 1 d 2 a 3 g 4 h 5 c 6 f 7 e
3 1 J 2 J 3 A 4 M 5 M 6 A 7 A 8 M
4 1 T 2 F 3 F 4 F 5 T 6 T 7 F 8 T
5 1 scene 2 first 3 just 4 next 5 happens 6 ridiculous 7 end
6 1 Anybody 2 Anything 3 Since 4 didn't 5 Afraid 6 have 7 course 8 problem
7 1 it wasn't the end of 2 didn't use to leave (never used to leave) 3 Hardly any adverts 4 isn't anything you say 5 were so many 6 was written 7 rather you didn't use 8 getting used to staying
8 1 series 2 many 3 such 4 only 5 sooner 6 However 7 all 8 sum
9 Students' own answers

Exam Choice 3

1 A
2 1 NI 2 F 3 T 4 F 5 F 6 NI 7 F 8 F
3 1 1890 2 Jefferson 3 the USA 4 $75 5 writer and director 6 *The Artist* 7 illness 8 strokes 9 answering letters and phone calls from fans 10 go skiing
4 1 opinion 2 Because 3 reason 4 mean 5 fact 6 put 7 way 8 right 9 recap
5 1 a 2 both 3 was 4 The 5 does 6 have 7 by 8 all 9 did 10 to
6 1 b 2 c 3 a 4 c 5 b 6 b
7 Students' own answers

Exam Choice 4

1 1 F 2 NI 3 T 4 F 5 NI 6 T 7 F 8 F
2 1 c 2 a 3 c 4 d
3 a 5 b 1 c 4 d 2 f 3
4 1 T 2 NI 3 T 4 F 5 NI
5 1 recommend 2 you 3 don't 4 not 5 advise 6 let's 7 rather 8 means 9 worth 10 point
6 1 to 2 It 3 there 4 what 5 who 6 have 7 watching 8 when (whenever) 9 no 10 where 11 which 12 were
7 1 a 2 c 3 a 4 b 5 c 6 c 7 b 8 a 9 c 10 a
8 Students' own answers

Exam Choice 5

1 1 G 2 C 3 F 4 A 5 B 6 E
2 1 NI 2 T 3 F 4 F 5 T 6 F 7 NI 8 F
3 1 north London 2 family's business 3 jeweller's 4 Directors 5 jokes 6 sandwich 7 five thousand 8 was sacked 9 four million
4 1 is 2 does 3 about 4 thing 5 would 6 what 7 best 8 with 9 it 10 be 11 another
5 1 international/multinational 2 unreliable 3 rebellious 4 colourful 5 voluntary 6 environmentally 7 creative 8 underused 9 useless 10 forbidden
6 1 in order to 2 Therefore 3 as 4 because 5 since 6 as a result 7 so that 8 to
7 Students' own answers

Online Skills 1

2 Aung San Suu Kyi was born in **1945** to an influential **Burmese** family. She … won the Nobel Peace Prize in **1991**.

Online Skills 2

2 1 b 2 a 3 c

Online Skills 3

2 a 5 b 3 d 4 e 6 f 2
4 a 2 b 4 c 5 e 3

Online Skills 5

1 1 c 2 a 3 c
2 1 F There was a fire in his lab before he could do it. 2 T 3 T 4 T 5 F He died just before the battle was won.

Pearson Education Limited
Edinburgh Gate
Harlow
Essex CM20 2JE
England
and Associated Companies throughout the world.

www.pearsonELT.com

First published 2013
Sixth impression 2019
ISBN: 978-1-4479-0167-9
Set in Neo Sans Std 9pt
Printed in Malaysia (CTP-VVP)

Acknowledgements

We are grateful to the following for permission to reproduce copyright material:

Figures
Figure M4.1 from http://www.thekitchn.com/product-review-zoku-quick-pop-119685; Figure M4.1 from http://www.pcmag.com/slideshow_viewer/0,3253,I%253D254843%2526a%253D254936%2526po%253D1,00.asp?p=n, www.mintcleaner.com; Figure M6.1 from The Murders in the Rue Morgue, Vintage Classics (Edgar Allan Poe), From The Murders in the Rue Morgue by Edgar Allan Poe Published by Vintage

In some instances we have been unable to trace the owners of copyright material, and we would appreciate any information that would enable us to do so.

Photo acknowledgements

The publisher would like to thank the following for their kind permission to reproduce their photographs:

(Key: b-bottom; c-centre; l-left; r-right; t-top)

Alamy Images: © Alex Segre 54, © Archimage 22b, Chris Ryan 24, DCPhoto 74, Douglas Peebles Photography 66t, © Hakbong Kwon 70b, Iain Masterton 88b, MBI 9, tony french 88t, vario images GmbH & Co.KG 29; **Corbis:** E.O. Hoppé 118, © Leif Skoogfors 83, © Michael S. Yamashita 82t; **Evolution Robotics - USA - www.mintcleaner.com:** 38b; **FotoLibra:** Kevin Hellon 70c; **Getty Images:** AFP / Getty Images 58, De Agostini 66 (background), Getty Images / Entertainment 110, Getty Images / Hulton Archive 22t, Getty Images / sport 48, iconics / a.collectionRF 52, MIXA 82b, Popperfoto 59, RyuheiShindo / Taxi 4, Time & Life Pictures / Getty Images 16l; **Juliette Brindak; Co-founder, Miss O & Friends; Photo: courtesy of Shape Magazine:** 92r; **Motycka Enterprises, LLC:** 92l; **Press Association Images:** AP 16r, KhinMaung Win / AP 114; **Rex Features:** Dan Sparham 70t, Ken McKay 96, Monkey Business Images 57, Rex Features 26, Sipa Press 104; **Shutterstock.com:** JoWay 117, Ramon Espelt Photography 84, shock 68; **SuperStock:** © Tetra Images 47; **The Kobal Collection:** SILVER PICTURES 116; **The Random House Group Ltd.:** 60; **www.zokuhome.com:** 38t

All other images © Pearson Education

Every effort has been made to trace the copyright holders and we apologise in advance for any unintentional omissions. We would be pleased to insert the appropriate acknowledgement in any subsequent edition of this publication.

Illustration acknowledgements

Illustrated by Kathy Baxendale pp 51, 102, 112; Stephen Dew pp 35, 79, 107; Mark Draisey pp 15, 64, 95; Bill Piggins pp 7, 28, 75, 101.

Cover images: Front: **Corbis:** Blend Images / Jon Feingersh cr; **Getty Images:** John W Banagan c, Digital Vision r, Fraser Hall cl; Shutterstock.com: Garsya l